Neil T. Jensen
3313 Churchill St.
Saint Paul, MN 55126

COWBOY
MOVIES

GALLERY BOOKS
An Imprint of W. H. Smith Publishers Inc.
112 Madison Avenue
New York City 10016
A Bison Book

COWBOY MOVIES

NORMAN V RICHARDS

*With love to my daughter, Gayle Richards Couch,
who provided most of the research for this book*

Published by Gallery Books
A Division of W.H. Smith Publishers Inc.
112 Madison Avenue
New York, New York 10016

Produced by
Bison Books Corp.
17 Sherwood Place
Greenwich, CT 06830
USA

Printed in Hong Kong

1 2 3 4 5 6 7 8 9 10

ISBN 0-8317-9405-4

CONTENTS

COWBOYS ON FILM

Western movies have been the most popular type of film since the birth of film making more than 80 years ago. More Westerns have been made than movies of any other genre and, undoubtedly, more people have seen them. Often derided as 'horse operas' and 'oaters,' the cowboy movies have had an amazingly durable and broad-based appeal, confounding some critics. Understanding this popularity requires some examination of the basic qualities of the Western story.

The Western story is the great American legend. The Greeks had their mythological heroes, England had its Camelot and its tales of Robin Hood, and America has its cowboy. The best-known symbol of American culture at home and abroad for nearly a century, the cowboy and the Western adventure have had an irresistible romantic

Page 1 : A man lies dead on a western bar room floor after a run-in with Gregory Peck, in *The Gunfighter*.
Pages 2–3 : John Wayne, as Rooster Cogburn, instructs Kim Darby in self-defense in *True Grit*.
Previous pages : In *Stagecoach*, Director John Ford showed breathtaking scenes of the coach moving across the windswept wastelands of Monument Valley, Utah.
Left : Dean Martin in a shoot-out in *Rio Bravo*.

Above : Ronald Reagan was a popular leading man, especially during the 1940s, before he was elected President of the United States. Here, in one of his few cowboy parts, he is suffering through an attempted stringing up in *Santa Fe Trail*. Lynchings or attempted lynchings seemed to be a common occurrence in Western films.

Opposite : Alan Ladd as Shane, a man who is a good-guy gunfighter who comes to town to shoot the bad-guy gunfighter, Jack Palance. Here he is seen with the hero-worshipping son of a ranch family he decides to protect, played by the outstanding child film star, Brandon de Wilde. *Shane* (1953) was photographed in color against the sweep of the Grand Tetons and shown on a wide screen, and tells the time-honored story of homesteaders struggling against a cattle baron who was out to take their lands away. Director George Stevens let the audience see the unfolding events through the eyes of the little son of the homesteaders.

appeal for people everywhere. The self-reliant man on horseback, the solitary hero who confronts the elements of a harsh land and the worst that human enemies can do, is regarded as a symbol of American character.

Beyond the obvious reasons for its appeal in movies and on television—spectacular outdoor settings, suspense, abundant action and violence—the Western legend appeals to something deeper in most of us. We like to relate ourselves to the attractive qualities embodied in the Western hero—qualities which represent a moral code of our culture.

Dr William W Savage Jr of the University of Oklahoma cites the common sense typically displayed by the Western hero. In his book, *The Cowboy Hero, His Image in American History and Culture*, he wrote, 'The cowboy's facility of mind explains much of his popularity in our culture, for Americans espouse nothing if not common sense. . . . He is popular because he, more than any single historical or mythical figure from America's past, represents the fine middle-class virtue of common sense, and in action at that.'

The solitary Western hero is also a seeker and a pilgrim, moving on, going somewhere, and searching within himself. He may be a drifter, but his search for self-identity strikes a responsive chord in many of us.

The cowboy represents the elements of the American character that are most admired: a lack of pretentiousness; a directness and democratic humility in speech; courage; honesty and the ability to settle problems decisively.

Beyond all else, the Western hero stands for freedom. His chosen environment, a vast, wild empire of desert, plains, rugged hills and mountains, is generally empty of all but a few settlers' cabins and wandering Indians. His ability to move where he wants, when he wants to, is unimpaired; he moves with the wind. Contrast that freedom of action with the lives and obligations most of us have today in our urbanized society and the enduring attraction of the cowboy symbol is understandable.

The physical toughness, self-reliance, sincerity and basic masculinity of the cowboy still attracts us, which may explain why western wear—a symbolic identification with the cowboy—is so popular in a transitional time that some observers say has undermined the male's image of himself.

The legendary cowboy hero also displays an integration of opposing tendencies in people, to which we can relate. The Western hero's courage is balanced by his modesty. Similarly, his capacity for physical violence, based on his strength and experience, is balanced and disciplined by his reluctance to resort to force. Only when there is no other way out does he settle problems with his six-shooter.

These qualities help account for the Western legend's lasting appeal. As a legend, it is just that—and not necessarily an accurate mirror of America's Western history. Some basic facts of the Western legend are true, of course, but they sometimes obstruct the greater reality of how the West was really won.

There was, indeed, a migration to the wilderness areas of the West in the 19th century; there was the establishment of cattle ranches and the long cattle drives to markets and railroad towns; it was common to see boisterous behavior by cowboys in towns like Dodge City and Abilene after long months on cattle drives; there was a need in some places for tough sheriffs and marshals to maintain order; there were some Indian battles and disputes between cattle ranchers and farmer-settlers. And undoubtedly some con men, gamblers and other undesirable types were attracted to certain Western towns to take advantage of new opportunities.

But many historians point out that these elements of the 'wild west' were the exception, rather than the rule, of everyday life during that period. Gunfights in the streets and saloons were not an everyday occurrence; most Western settlers didn't wear guns. The vast majority of people who settled the West led prosaic, hard-working lives farming the land, raising cattle and sheep, building homes and establishing businesses. It was a rare Westerner who suffered Indian raids, saw gunfights in the streets or watched pitched battles between posses and outlaw gangs. The violence was there, but probably in no greater measure than is the case in our present society. The standard conflicts that are so much a part of the Western legend simply didn't typify life for most people in the West; they read about these wild happenings occasionally in their newspapers.

But the true history of most people's experiences in settling the West is not the stuff of which romantic legends are made. It was necessary for a gifted story teller to seize on the dramatic (if uncommon) aspects of Western life and embellish them mightily to excite the popular imagination. Such a man was Edward Z C Judson, a writer better known by his pen name, Ned Buntline. A New Yorker, Judson had experienced some adventures in his own somewhat shady life. He had run away to sea at 13, later escaped a lynch mob in Tennessee after shooting and killing a man over a woman, and had served a year in jail for inciting a riot in New York. But he had also been a successful writer during all this, and he went West to find new subjects to write about.

He quickly found one when he met William F Cody, a man who had led a far more adventurous life in the West than the average cowboy or sheriff. He had been a wagon driver, Pony Express rider, buffalo hunter and had teamed with Wild Bill Hickok as an Indian fighter. He had earned a genuine reputation for bravery in battle as a scout and Indian fighter with the US Army Fifth Cavalry, distinguishing himself in nine battles. And he had accomplished all this while still a young man. He was 23 when Judson met him and was easily the most colorful character the author had ever seen. The roistering Cody was fond of marathon drinking bouts, knew he was handsome ('vain as a woman at Easter', someone said) and loved the attention his exploits created. He favored white buckskin suits, scarlet shirts and a white sombrero over his shoulder-length hair.

The two men hit if off immediately. Judson interviewed

Above: Charles Starrett comes sailing out of the jail, six-guns blazing, in *Texas Dynamo*. When Tim McCoy left Columbia Studios, several contract players at the studio were tested to be his replacement. The winner was Starrett. From 1935 to 1952, Starrett made 132 Westerns for them.

Top: A scene from *Dodge City*. Errol Flynn looks in on the jailed Guinn 'Big Boy' Williams. The film was a story of a town in Kansas in the days when the railroads were heading west. Colonel Dodge of Dodge City sums up the railroad as 'a symbol of America's progress—iron horses and iron men.' He added, 'the West stands for honesty, courage and morality.' Flynn is the embodiment of these qualities, and, flanked by Williams and Alan Hale, he confronts the crooked machinations of Bruce Cabot and Victor Jory. Flynn is a wagonmaster and his bar-room brawl in the film was a masterpiece. As a lead-in to the next picture, Dodge enlists Flynn to help clean up another town. The film was *Virginia City*.

Cody about a recent exploit in which Cody had killed an Indian chief in hand-to-hand combat before witnesses who swore to his bravery. Then the writer went back East and wrote *Buffalo Bill, the King of the Bordermen,* the first of 557 'dime novels' that he and others would produce about a Western hero named Buffalo Bill. Thus christened Buffalo Bill, Cody was launched on a spectacular career that would make him one of the most famous Americans of his time, earn him huge amounts of money for many years, and turn the American West into a legend throughout the world.

In a few short years, Buntline's dime novels (and those of his imitators) turned the popular conception of the West into the 'Wild West'—a gaudy, romantic, action-packed saga of irresistible appeal. A larger-than-life character like Cody hardly needed any embellishment in print, but the Ned Buntline novels went far beyond the truth, describing such superhuman feats and derring-do by Buffalo Bill that Cody didn't recognize himself in them. (What probably amazed Cody most was one novel in which he was portrayed as a noble champion of temperance, when in actuality his drinking habits were a legend in themselves.)

Never one to quibble about exaggeration though, whether about himself or the 'Wild West,' Cody soon realized the opportunities that his sudden fame presented. In 1872, Judson wrote a play about Buffalo Bill's exploits and talked Cody into playing himself in the melodrama. The play was a hit in Chicago, Boston, New York and other cities; Cody's fame escalated and so did the public's perception of the West as a wildly romantic, adventurous place peopled by flamboyant, war-painted Indians and white men like Cody. After several years of appearing in other melodramas about himself, Cody organized the first of his famous Buffalo Bill Wild West shows—a sort of circus attraction with exciting action. A natural showman, he packed thrills into every show, using real Indians, cowboys, buffalo and horses. He featured simulated buffalo hunts, roundups, bucking broncos and exhibitions of trick shooting. The shows starred Sitting Bull himself and Annie Oakley, the famed woman sharpshooter. Cody's version of life in the 'Wild West' played for many years all over the United States and in Europe, where it was immensely popular. England's Queen Victoria became one of Cody's most ardent fans and he received an audience with Pope Leo XIII at the Vatican.

Buffalo Bill's shows and Ned Buntline's dime novels managed to distill the American West into a few vivid symbols—the cowboy, the Indian, the buffalo, the stagecoach, the expert shot, fast on the draw—which became standard metaphors for all writers and film makers thereafter.

With the publication of Owen Wister's novel, *The Virginian,* in 1902, more serious writers began to treat the Western legend in literature. Wister's novel helped establish another staple of the Western: the strong, silent hero who travels alone and is fast with a gun. His lead character's

Above: The second version of Owen Wister's *The Virginian* starred Gary Cooper and Mary Bryan. It had been filmed previously with Dustin Farnum and later with Joel McCrae.

Top: The *Iron Horse* was directed by John Ford and was one of the earliest movies made exclusively on location. The picture was about the building of the transcontinental railroad and starred George O'Brien. About 6000 extras were used.

famous remark, 'When you call me that, smile' set the tone for generations of cowboy heroes to follow.

Thomas A Edison had barely perfected his invention of the motion picture camera when the Western theme became a subject. Before there were movie screens, one-minute reels of film were shown in arcades on kinetoscopes or 'peep show' machines. There were no plots, of course, in these short vignettes, but the makers knew that anything Western would be popular, thanks to the enthusiasm created by Buffalo Bill's shows and the dime novels. They showed reconstructions of what were thought to be typical Western incidents: a cattle roundup, a stagecoach holdup, an Indian raid. Buffalo Bill Cody also appeared in the new medium. It is interesting to note that as these first Western movies appeared, just before the turn of the century, Butch Cassidy and his gang were still robbing banks and trains on horseback out West. A short time later, a real frontier lawman, the famed William M Tilghman, directed a Western movie which included in its cast an authentic Western bank robber, Al Jennings, just released from jail.

The move from these brief vignettes on 'peep show' machines to complete Western stories came with *The Great Train Robbery*, produced by Edison's company in 1903. This film, photographed and directed in New Jersey by an Edison employee, Edwin S Porter, ran a full 10 minutes.

Opposite top : The beginning of the crime in *The Great Train Robbery*. The robbers draw their guns on the railroad telegraph operator. They will bind and gag him so that he cannot send for help while they take over the train that is stopping for more water for the engine.

Opposite bottom : Gilbert Maxwell 'Broncho Billy' Anderson (1882–1971), an unsuccessful vaudeville performer who drifted into films in *The Great Train Robbery* (1903). He later founded the Essanay company and made nearly 400 one-reel Westerns starring himself. Anderson was given a special Academy Award in 1957 'for his contribution to the development of motion pictures.'

Below : William S Hart, shown here taking a director's view of one of his own action-packed films, was a creative genius in the Western genre, and one of the most famous performers in the 1920s. His middle initial was reported to have stood for either 'Shakespeare' or 'Surrey.'

Its plot helped set the formula for countless Westerns to follow: a crime is committed; the heroes pursue the villains; a showdown occurs and justice prevails. The story included the sure-fire appeal of action: fistfights, shooting with six-guns, pursuit on horseback and even saloon bullies shooting bullets into the floor to make a 'dude' dance. *The Great Train Robbery* was a remarkably good film for its time.

It was several years before more development of the Western took place. A budding film maker and actor named G M Anderson, who had played small parts in *The Great Train Robbery* and other Westerns, gave the genre the lift it needed and became the first movie cowboy hero. He filmed a short Western called *Broncho Billy and the Baby* in 1908, and since he couldn't find an actor to play the part of the hero, he played it himself. The film was a huge success; the public liked his portrayal of the solitary hero with a heart of gold. The name stuck, and Broncho Billy Anderson went on to make and star in hundreds of short features. His films have been described as the ancestors of the 'B' Westerns that came later, appealing mainly to children. His simple plots were strong and direct, and he made his films in California, which provided authentic Western settings. Soon children all over the country (and not a few adults) were flocking to see Broncho Billy Anderson movies, and he reigned supreme on the Western scene for several years until a major rival overtook him in popularity.

That rival was William S Hart, a mature Shakespearean stage actor who went on to become a major force in shaping the Western movie. The very embodiment of the strong, silent Western hero, Hart added new depth of story and characterization to his films, many of which he directed. He was the guiding spirit behind all his movies, lifting them to an adult level of interest.

Despite his Eastern stage training, Hart had an authentic Western background. He had spent much of his youth on the frontier, had known the Indian and the true cowboy, and was a friend of such lawmen as Wyatt Earp and Bat Masterson. Hart had a genuine love for the West and tried to show the *true* romance and harsh beauty of the frontier through gritty realism in his films.

Arriving in Hollywood in 1914 (it had become established as the center for filmmaking by then), Hart began making Westerns for producer Thomas Ince, who, along with D W Griffith, was responsible for many of the best Westerns made during that period of development. Ince gave Hart a great deal of freedom to develop the kind of Western Hart believed in, and it paid off. Hart became one of the biggest stars in movies and Ince profited handsomely over a period of years. Hart established his own stock company of actors, writers, cameramen and sometimes directors to pursue his vision of the West on film.

His films were of almost documentary quality, rather than glamorized, for he insisted on a kind of hard realism. His Western towns were weatherbeaten and rundown, his characters wore dingy clothes and had authentic-looking frontier faces, and there were clouds of dust in the streets

13

and on the range. Later directors lost some of this dusty authenticity by wetting the ground to make riding scenes clearer, but Hart wanted realism all the way. There were no fancy-looking cowboys in fringed shirts in his films; everyone looked as if they worked hard eking out a living on the frontier.

His stories depended more on characterization and strong story lines with moral themes than on action. While he limited the action, Hart embellished his plots with a great deal of his personal sentimentality. His attitude of old-fashioned chivalry toward women showed up again and again in his movies. His hero was often an outlaw who is reformed after meeting the heroine and who performs a number of self-sacrificing and brave deeds to prove his worth to her.

During the first few years of Hart's career, his strong plots and realism were fresh and original, but in the later years, the sentimental qualities of his stories repeated themselves too much, slowing down the action. Hart didn't believe in action for its own sake, but when he did use it, he was good at it, both as a director and as an actor. He was already 44 years old when he began making films, but he did all his own hard riding and fight scenes to the end of his career, when he was 56.

Hart's films were all made in the silent era with primitive equipment by today's standards, and none of his movies could measure up to the great Westerns made since the advent of sound—*Stagecoach*, *High Noon*, *Shane* and other classics. But for his time, he was probably the best maker of Westerns, and his last film, *Tumbleweeds*, still stands as a good, big, epic Western. Made in 1925, it featured spectacular scenes of the Oklahoma land rush which still look good today, even though they were filmed without the fluid camera movement now possible with huge mobile camera cranes and other equipment now available to directors.

Hart's retirement was hastened by a competitor who overtook him in popularity with a new approach to Westerns: Tom Mix. This new cowboy hero didn't care as much about historical realism and depth of plots—he was convinced the public would flock to see films loaded with action scenes, however implausible they might be. And he was right: Mix's streamlined, fast-moving, all-action movies quickly caught the fancy of the public, especially youngsters. Wearing flamboyant fringed shirts, big white hats and hand-tooled boots, Tom Mix (along with his famed horse, Tony) became the new favorite with movie goers in the mid-20s. By contrast, Hart's more realistic Westerns seemed slow-moving and old-fashioned. When his producers urged him to change the style of his films to keep up with Mix, Hart refused. With the field left open to him, Tom Mix went on to become perhaps the most famous movie cowboy hero of all time.

Born in Mix Run, Pennsylvania, Tom Mix had led an adventurous life before he ever reached Hollywood. He served in the army, worked on Western ranches, and had been a champion rodeo rider and performer with the

A trio of cowboy stars of the 1920s and 1930s.

Above: Tom Mix (1880–1940) who made over 400 low-budget Westerns.

Opposite top: Hoot Gibson (1892–1962), who had actually been a cowboy. He specialized in good-humored Westerns.

Opposite bottom: Ken Maynard (1895–1973), who was once a rodeo rider and then worked in films as a stunt man.

Miller Brothers Ranch Show. He had not done many of the things credited to him later by movie studio publicists, however: he had not fought in the Spanish-American War, the Philippine insurrection or the Boer War, and he had not been an active Texas Ranger and sheriff. But his expertise as a rodeo rider stood him in good stead for the type of action movies he was to make.

From 1911 to 1917, Mix toiled in almost a hundred short Western films for an obscure studio called Selig. These shorts were mediocre at best, but Mix had the chance in many of them to serve as writer, director and star, thus building experience in filmmaking. He used them to display his prowess at riding and stunting, and eventually these qualities caught the collective eye of Fox studio executives. In 1917 Mix went to work at Fox, then the largest studio in Hollywood, and proceeded to earn immense profits for them.

A special formula was devised for Tom Mix Westerns. The hero was the epitome of clean living; he neither drank nor smoked in his movies. (This set a pattern for cowboy heroes which was followed by many others.) The plots were simple, with no serious or thoughtful issues presented. The main ingredient was action, with many chases and fights throughout each feature film. But Mix's heroes hardly ever shot and killed the villains; they were subdued with fists or by roping. The aim, of course, was to appeal to youngsters. Since action was more important than logic, Mix arranged many stunts in these films, most of which he performed himself rather than using professional stuntmen, as was more common.

It took a few years, but by the mid-20s, Mix was at the top of his class, the most popular cowboy hero in America. He remained there for another 10 years, grinding out films which could lay no claim to greatness but which were immensely popular. An entire generation of children grew up knowing Tom Mix as the greatest cowboy hero in the world. Along the way, the flamboyant Mix established the formula for the many hundreds of 'B' Westerns that were made in the decades to follow.

Anything successful is quickly imitated in Hollywood, and Mix's formula of action-packed adventures by a hero in fancy dress was copied in great numbers. Fox and all the other studios developed cowboy heroes and put them in numerous Westerns based on the Tom Mix formula. Buck Jones, George O'Brien and others advanced from extra roles to leading men and developed their own followings. Veteran Western actors such as Hoot Gibson, Fred Thomson, Ken Maynard, Tim McCoy and Yakima Canutt cashed in on the new formula Mix had established, grinding out great numbers of horse operas for Saturday afternoon matinees.

The advent of sound in motion pictures helped create a new boom in Westerns in the 30s. In an effort to stimulate box office success during the Depression, double bills (two movies for the price of one ticket) became standard at theaters. To fill this increased demand for films, studios turned out great numbers of low-budget or 'B' movies—

detective thrillers, comedies and Westerns—to accompany the 'A' movies, or main attractions.

Most of the Western stars from the silent era made the transition to these low-budget sound films. Tom Mix, Buck Jones, Ken Maynard, Tim McCoy, George O'Brien and others soon had series of their own in sound. In addition, John Wayne, Randolph Scott and other actors who would later go on to starring in quality 'A' Westerns, broke into the 'B' Westerns in the 30s.

Most of the studios produced the 'B' Westerns, but Universal, Monogram and Republic specialized in them, turning out hundreds. There was room enough for more cowboy stars, and they soon developed: Charles Starrett, Johnny Mack Brown, Bob Steele, Tex Ritter, William Boyd (as Hopalong Cassidy) and scores of lesser-known actors became active in Westerns. These cheaply made movies offered little variation from the Tom Mix formula, but they went on making money year after year.

The next significant development in the Western began in 1935, when Republic made *Tumbling Tumbleweeds*, starring Gene Autry. This former radio singer wasn't the first cowboy to sing in a movie, but he was the first to make a huge hit with his singing. The public response was electrifying, and the studio quickly devised a new formula for singing cowboy movies. Autry's genial personality and pleasant, unpretentious singing style soon propelled him into the top range of box office stars. The singing cowboy movie had, of course, even less connection with historical reality than did the Tom Mix formula, and the studios didn't pretend that it was plausible. Autry's films were

Above : Marlene Dietrich was one of the few true screen goddesses to star in a Western film—*The Spoilers* (1942). Here John Wayne eyes Randolph Scott suspiciously as Dietrich merely smiles. *The Spoilers*, based upon a Rex Beach novel, has been filmed five times—in 1914, 1922, 1930, 1942 and 1956. Dietrich had previously been in another Western—*Destry Rides Again* (1939), with James Stewart.

Opposite top : Johnny Mack Brown (standing) was a Western star who was a former All-American football player. He also made a few non-Westerns, co-starring with such female luminaries as Mary Pickford, Joan Crawford and Greta Garbo.

Opposite bottom : At the end of a fight, Gene Autry stares down at his victim in *Sioux City Sue*. Autry, an easy-going Texan, made millions in films from 1935 to 1954 as a singing cowboy, usually with his horse, Champion. Today he is still wealthy, most notably as the owner of the California Angels baseball team.

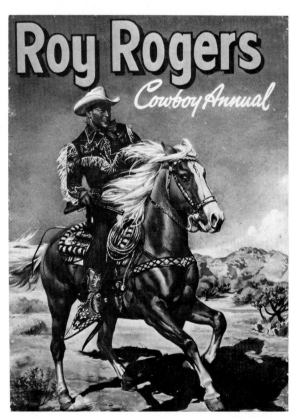

Top : Roy Rogers, 'The King of the Cowboys,' born Leonard Slye in Cincinnati, Ohio in 1912. Early in his career, he formed the 'Sons of the Pioneers' Western singing group. He was one of the top Western stars from 1938 to 1953, and usually appeared with his horse, Trigger, and often with his wife, Dale Evans. Today, one of his enterprises is a chain of fast-food restaurants.

Above : Roy Rogers was popular in many parts of the world. This is the cover of a boy's book published in Britain in the early 1950s.

Above : Gordon 'Wild Bill' Elliott, a burly leading man of films in the 1920s, who went on to be a popular star of low-budget Westerns. Born Gordon Nance, he was one of the few real actors to become cowboy stars, having studied at the Pasadena (California) Playhouse.

about modern times and he often played a rodeo or radio star who got involved in fighting some cheating businessmen, politicians or other 'bad guys.' The incongruity of Autry and the other actors riding horses and wearing six-guns while battling villains in cars and airplanes didn't seem to bother his fans. He always had his comic sidekick (usually Smiley Burnette) and his songs to disarm any viewer criticism.

Autry's great box office success naturally produced singing cowboys from everywhere. Tex Ritter, Bob Baker, Jack Randall, Smith Ballew, James Newill, Fred Scott and Dick Foran copied Autry's formula in the 30s. In the 40s, Jimmy Wakely, Rex Allen, Monte Hale and Eddie Dean all emerged as would-be successors to Autry. The only one who ever challenged Autry's popularity, of course, was Roy Rogers, who had played small parts in some Autry films. After Autry joined the military service in World War II, Rogers, who managed to stay home, was given a big publicity buildup as 'King of the Cowboys.' He went on to a long and highly successful career in movies, television and personal appearances with his wife, Dale Evans. No other singing cowboys came close to matching Autry and Rogers, who influenced the 'B' Westerns for years. Taking Tom Mix's flashy clothes several steps further (particularly Rogers, who usually looked like a member of a Broadway chorus line), they planted the belief in a couple of generations of children that cowboys wore rhinestones and unbelievably gaudy clothes to work—not that they were often seen working in their movies. But the kids loved them, and why not? They provided very pleasant entertainment on countless Saturday afternoons.

The 'B' Westerns continued to be made throughout the 40s and into the 50s, when competition from television finally killed them. During the 40s such stars as Sunset Carson, Wild Bill Elliott, Don 'Red' Barry, George Montgomery, Tim Holt, Lash LaRue, Whip Wilson and numerous others flourished in the 'B' Westerns. Duncan Renaldo and then Gilbert Roland played in the 'Cisco Kid' series, and Charles Starrett was 'The Durango Kid' in dozens of action-packed films.

Curiously, despite the advantages of sound capability, Hollywood studios virtually ignored the big, epic or 'A' Western during the 30s. With only a few exceptions, Westerns were regarded as low-status potboilers and not worthy of big budgets and big stars. About the only major star who occasionally appeared in Westerns was Gary Cooper, who made his sound picture debut in *The Virginian* and went on to star in both Westerns and other types of films.

It took the genius of director John Ford finally to develop Hollywood's capabilities for first-class Westerns. Ford had started directing 'B' Westerns and shorts in the silent film days. He made his mark in 1924 by making one of the best epic Westerns of that era, *The Iron Horse*. But after one more Western, he abandoned the genre for some 13 years, until he made *Stagecoach*, the landmark film

Top : Don 'Red' Barry was another popular star of Grade 'B' Westerns. Here he is in *Wyoming Wildcat*. He came to Hollywood after several years of stage experience. Later he broke away from Westerns and appeared as a featured actor in many big-budget films.

Above : The Cisco Kid, played by Duncan Renaldo, in *Valiant Hombre*. Renaldo had been in big-budget films ranging from *Trader Horn* (1930) to *For Whom the Bell Tolls* (1942), then became more famous with the Cisco Kid films.

which brought respectability to Westerns in 1939. This super-Western starred John Wayne and rescued him from a long stretch in 'B' Westerns. It also showed the potential for quality, big-budget productions in the Western genre and spurred an era of a quarter-century during which Hollywood made its finest Westerns.

Ford shot virtually all his films on location, getting authenticity and beautiful backgrounds that were impossible on back lots. He expanded the use of high cranes and other mobile equipment to gain panoramic scenes that gave the feeling of spaciousness essential to Western epics. And his plots were serious stories, aimed at adult audiences rather than children, and filled with historical authenticity.

Working with John Wayne in many of his films, Ford made a more consistently high-quality group of Westerns in his career than any other director. *My Darling Clementine, She Wore a Yellow Ribbon, The Wagon Master, Fort Apache, Rio Grande, The Searchers, The Horse Soldiers, Sergeant Rutledge, Two Rode Together, The Man Who Shot Liberty Valance, How the West Was Won* and *Cheyenne Autumn* are some of his superior body of work extending from the 30s through the 60s. Individual Western classics made by other directors—*Red River, Shane, High Noon* and others—might outrank Ford pictures in the eyes of some critics, but for consistent quality over the years, Ford stands alone.

Above: A scene from a monumental Western—*Stagecoach* (1939). Left to right: John Carradine, Andy Devine, Chris-Pin Martin, George Bancroft, Louis Platt, Donald Meek, Claire Trevor, John Wayne, Berton Churchill. The film had everything—the birth of a baby, cut telegraph lines, an attack by Indians, a chase, a cavalry rescue, a poker game, a three-against-one gunfight and a happy ending.

Opposite top: In *My Darling Clementine* (1946) Henry Fonda played Wyatt Earp and Linda Darnell played Doc Holliday's girl. The locale of the picture was Tombstone, Arizona, where Earp was marshal, and the film culminated with the oft-photographed gunfight at the OK Corral.

Opposite bottom: In *My Darling Clementine* Henry Fonda was Wyatt Earp and Victor Mature was Doc Holliday. Fonda had made another Western, *The Ox-Bow Incident*, three years before, and then punctuated his remarkable career with Western roles.

20

Above : Gunfighter Nate Champion (Christopher Walken) fights for his life in a shootout in front of his cabin in Michael Cimino's *Heaven's Gate* (1980), one of the biggest box office disasters in the history of Western films. It was re-released in 1983 in a slightly longer form and was better received both by the critics and the public.

Opposite : John Wayne played the part of a rugged commander of a cavalry outpost in *She Wore a Yellow Ribbon* (1949). Although undermanned, he is forced to drive invading Indians back north. The director was John Ford—the master of the Western movie. At left, holding the flag is the young Ben Johnson, who, 22 years later, won an Academy Award for another picture that has been classified as a Western— but a modern Western—*The Last Picture Show.*

The era which saw Hollywood produce its finest Westerns—the 40s, 50s and 60s—was the last in which many Westerns were produced. Few are made today, but as the cycles of public taste turn, we can expect a real possibility of a resurgence in Westerns in the years to come. The great Westerns made in the 40s, 50s and 60s—and even a few in the 70s—offered mature themes, superb characterization, superior photography and historical authenticity. They attracted some of the finest actors, many of whom did not specialize in Westerns but who recognized good stories and strong characters. Henry Fonda, Marlon Brando, James Stewart, Paul Newman, Charlton Heston, Burt Lancaster, Gregory Peck, Robert Mitchum, Clark Gable, Kirk Douglas and countless other top stars used the Western genre to good advantage as vehicles for their talent.

As recently as 1980, one of the most ambitious attempts in film history was made on a Western movie. Director Michael Cimino spent an estimated $35 to $45 million to make *Heaven's Gate*, which ran nearly four hours with an intermission and was a huge flop at the box office. The film, which centered on the Johnson County wars of Wyoming in the 1890s, contained striking photography but a vague, weak story line. Critics assailed *Heaven's Gate* unmercifully, and the project cost United Artists a great deal when the public stayed away from this attempted super-Western.

Not all the Westerns made from the 40s on were great, but enough were excellent to set high standards which we have come to expect. The next section of this book offers recollections of some of the films which made cinema history and established the legend of the American West in the eyes of the world for all time.

THE SILENT WESTERNS

Starting with one-minute films for 'peep show' machines, the vast majority of Westerns in the silent film era remained short subjects—one and two reels to accompany the main feature movies in theaters. Some of these short films were continuing episodes in serial form. The episode would end with the hero in a precarious situation; the viewers were enticed to return to the theater the following week to see the outcome.

Most of the Westerns in this period were far from works of art. In fact, they were ground out in simple, unimaginative formulas that provided plenty of action and little plot. The films of Broncho Billy Anderson and later Tom Mix fell into this simplistic category, aimed at children. The plots always contained villains committing crimes and the hero pursuing and fighting them until justice triumphed. They were virtually indistinguishable from one another and it would be impractical to single out any for review.

Left : In *The Covered Wagon* (1923) the wagons form a circle. This big-scale pioneer Western did much to establish the form. It ran more than two hours, following a wagon train of the mid-1800s westward across the deserts, plains and mountains, enduring hostile Indians, swollen rivers and blazing heat along the way. The picture was made on location in rugged Nevada and Utah country, and has become a classic.

On the other hand, William S Hart tried to portray realism and real stories in his films. While his results were uneven, his better efforts stand as milestones in the development of Western movies. The same might be said of the relatively small number of larger, 'epic' Westerns that filmmakers attempted in those years. Following are descriptions of some films which stand as examples of the development of Westerns in the silent era.

The Great Train Robbery (1903)

Technically, this was not the first Western movie, but it was the first to combine the basic Western elements and story into the form we recognize as the Western movie today. Produced by Thomas A Edison's company, it was directed by Edwin S Porter and filmed in New Jersey. The Edison company had produced a number of short Western vignettes, including at least one with Buffalo Bill Cody himself in it, prior to *The Great Train Robbery*. But this was the first attempt to tell a complete Western story over a span of ten minutes (almost a reel of film).

The achievement was remarkable for 1903; director Porter had no precedents to help him, yet he fashioned a complete story shown visually, without subtitles. His camera shots showed good composition, and in editing the film, he cut smoothly from interior shots to exterior and back again. He also succeeded in building dramatic tension into his film by intelligent editing.

The opening scene of the film takes place in the interior of a railroad telegraph office (actually a movie set). Then Porter superimposed footage of a train arriving, so that it is seen through a window of the station.

Some bandits hold up the operator at gunpoint, then tie him. The next scene, shot outside, shows the bandits boarding the train. Then the scene shifts to the interior of the train's express car (shot in a studio). Such shifting of scenes was virtually unheard-of in 1903, when films were usually shot on a single set, like a play. But Porter used the technique effectively, shifting again in his next scene to the moving train, where he placed his camera on the rear of the tender to shoot inside the locomotive. The bandits arrive and overpower the engineers after a hard fight; then dummies representing the engineers are thrown off the train in

Some scenes from *The Great Train Robbery* (1903).

Top : After overpowering the train crew, the villians force an engineer to uncouple the engine from the train.

Right : The telegraph operator has been tied up by the bandits, but is discovered by his daughter, who, after saying a prayer, releases him.

Opposite top : Robbing the mail car.

Opposite bottom : After the robbery, the crooks steal the engine and ride to where their horses are and ride off through the forest. Later they are captured by a posse that has been recruited after the telegraph operator reports the crime.

another smoothly executed sequence. The bandits escape in the train after stealing their loot, and halt the train further up the track. Then a long, panning shot shows them running into some woods.

Having shown the crime, the film now changes to portraying the forces of the law. A child (the telegraph operator's daughter) comes into the telegraph office and unties her father. The film next cuts to a dance hall or saloon, shot on a studio set, where a dance is in progress. An Eastern 'greenhorn' or 'dude' is forced to 'dance' by bullying cowboys who shoot at the floor, causing him to jump around. This extra bit of plot helps round out the Western story and also builds suspense, because the audience is certain that the telegraph operator will soon arrive with news of the robbery. A posse is quickly formed and sets out after the bandits.

The rest of the film concentrates on the chase and the defeat of the bandits. It shows the robbers dividing the spoils in their hideout, then the lawmen attacking them by surprise. The lawmen win, of course. The New Jersey scenery hardly looks Western, and the Eastern actors were not good riders, so the riding and other physical action are not very authentic. Nevertheless, *The Great Train Robbery* set the pattern—the crime, the chase, the fight, the victory of the 'good guys'—for thousands of Westerns to follow. It was an original, and Porter's creativity set a standard for movie makers at a very early stage. He even devised a sure-fire thrill for audiences to keep them talking about the film: a closeup in which a bandit fires his pistol directly at the camera. People screamed and fainted at this startling trick. *The Great Train Robbery* cost only $150 to make, and it was an instant box-office success, proving there was money to be made from filmmaking.

There were no stars or any single hero in this film; groups of men acted as the lawmen and the bandits. This essential part of the Western movie—the lone hero—didn't come until later, when Broncho Billy Anderson (who played several bit parts in *The Great Train Robbery*) established the cowboy hero. But the Western groundwork was laid in this remarkable film of 1903.

Hell's Hinges (1916)

This silent film represents one of Western hero William S Hart's most successful efforts. It also typifies Hart's approach to portraying the West. Hart ran the show on his movies; he was the guiding spirit behind the scripts, the camera work and the acting. And he had a personal vision of Westerns that remained the same in all his films. He believed in an earthy realism, showing real, hardworking cowboys and settlers and dusty, run-down towns. He wanted no glamorization of the real West (unlike Tom Mix with his fancy clothes) and he wanted real stories and human characters.

This is to Hart's credit, but it was balanced with his overly sentimental ideas about plots and characters as well as his rigidity in sticking to the same type of stories in all his

films. He used subtitles not only for his flowery dialogue, but for overblown, sentimental narrative description. By today's standards, the subtitles on Hart's films would be considered hilariously funny. But it must be remembered that he was communicating with audiences in an age far removed from our own, both in time and in speech customs.

The hero played by Hart was invariably a kind of 'good bad man'—a tough loner who had killed men or had gotten into trouble, but who had a streak of decency buried beneath his tough exterior. This type of Hart character became a staple of many later Westerns, of course (one is reminded of *Shane* and others). But Hart's character was always reformed by his relationship with a pretty woman. The plots hardly varied: the heroine would look upon Hart as a ruffian and a scoundrel; he would be smitten by her in a chivalrous way; he would perform various heroic and selfless deeds to redeem himself in her eyes. Hart's penchant for idealizing women showed itself in every film he made, and he expressed this to the audience right from the start of each movie.

This can be seen by reviewing some of the subtitles in *Hell's Hinges*, which featured excellent photography and was a superior Western for its time. The film opens in the East, where a young minister is being sent to the West by his superiors. They want to rescue him from the temptations of big city life, because, as a subtitle tells the audience, he is *A weak and selfish youth, utterly unfit for the calling.* The minister and his sister, Faith, are shown arriving in a desolate Western town soon afterward. A subtitle refers to it as *The town known on the government surveyor's maps as Placer Centre, but throughout the sun-baked territory as just plain 'Hell's Hinges', and a good place to 'ride wide of' . . . a gun-fighting, man-killing, devil's den of iniquity that scorched even the sun-parched soil on which it stood.*

The decent people in this town who welcome the new minister make up a tiny minority of the population. Most of the inhabitants are rowdy, dishonest, undesirable people who let a villain run their town. The villain, the subtitle shows, is *Silk Miller, mingling the oily craftiness of a Mexican with the deadly treachery of a rattler, no man's open enemy, and no man's friend.*

Top left : William S Hart in the center of a group of low-lifes in *Hell's Hinges* (1916). Hart, though he hailed from Newburgh, New York, was the first westerner to win stardom in a cowboy costume. He spent his boyhood in the Blackfoot and Sioux lands of Minnesota and Wisconsin. He had learned the Sioux language by the time he was six, and later in his teens worked as a ranch hand.

Bottom left : In *Hell's Hinges*, an unruly mob from a saloon kills the town preacher. Following this scene, Hart marches to the saloon, kicks the doors open and shouts, according to the subtitles, 'Hell needs this town, and it's goin' back, and goin' damn quick.'

Miller wants the new minister run out of town and he gives the job to William S Hart, who is introduced in a subtitle as *Blaze Tracey, the embodiment of the best and worst of the early West. A man-killer whose philosophy of life is summed up in the creed: shoot first and do your disputin' afterwards.*

But when Tracey meets Faith, the minister's sister, he is bowled over by her beauty and her purity. She looks at him with *a different kind of smile, sweet, honest and trustful, and seeming to say, 'How do you do, friend!'* Hart is shown looking a little remorseful in a close-up.

Tracey decides not to run Faith's brother out of town, but he doesn't do anything to protect him when a mob of townspeople mocks and yells at the minister. The following Sunday, however, the goodness buried in Tracey begins to emerge. When he enters a barn where the minister is trying to hold a service, he finds a crowd of bullies terrorizing the minister and his small flock of church folk. But Faith stands piously singing a hymn *like the eternal flame that shone over the blood-drenched Roman arena* as drunken ne'er-do-wells shout insults and fire their guns in the air. At this, Tracey draws his two guns and announces to the bullies: *'I'm announcing here and now that there ain't goin' to be no more pickin' on the parson's herd so long as they mind their own business'.*

The unruly mob quiets down; then Tracey turns to Faith and says, *'I reckon God ain't wantin' me much, Ma'am, but when I look at you, I feel I've been ridin' the wrong trail.'*

This was probably followed by convulsive piano music in the theater.

After this point, the action picks up as Tracey devotes himself to the cause of Good instead of Evil. The oily, crafty Silk Miller isn't about to give up. He tells his mistress, Dolly, to seduce the preacher after plying him with liquor. Dolly is quite effective at tasks of this sort. When she and the minister are lying drunk in her bed, Miller brings Tracey into the room and shows him, hoping to win him back to his side. But Tracey is incorruptible now, thanks to the pure Faith, and he rides off to seek medical help for the poor parson. But while he's doing this, an unruly mob from the saloon carries the inebriated preacher to the church. A fight breaks out there, the minister is killed and the church burns to the ground.

Tracey gallops back and finds Faith weeping over the preacher's body. With a look of cold fury and righteous indignation, Tracey marches to the saloon, kicks the doors open and shouts *'Hell needs this town, and it's goin' back, and goin' damn quick!'*

With eyes and guns ablaze, Tracey shoots the villain and cows his henchmen, none of whom dare draw their weapons. With an air of chivalry, the hero lets the dance-hall girls run out through the doorway before he shoots the saloon's kerosene lamps and sets the whole building aflame. The fire quickly spreads and the whole town burns to the ground.

Dawn comes, announced by a subtitle: *And then from the mothering sky came the baby dawn, singing as it wreathed*

Laying the golden spike in *The Iron Horse* (1924). John Ford traced the building of the Union Pacific Railroad in the film.

the gray horns of the mountains with ribbons of rose and gold. Tracey wanders to the cemetery and there is Faith, weeping over her brother's fresh grave. She and Tracey look meaningfully at each other, then stroll, side by side, toward sunlit mountain peaks in the distance. The final subtitle intones: *Whatever the future, theirs to share together.*

Despite the excess of sentimentality, by today's standards, *Hell's Hinges* is still regarded as one of the classic Westerns by many film historians. It was a landmark in 1916, an example of beautiful camera work and intelligent direction. It had a dusty realism as well as a feeling of a spectacle, especially in the scene where the town burns down, which was brilliantly staged. The camera angles were imaginative and the entire visual effect of the film was superb, thanks to Hart's vision as a director. His fame as an actor obscured his ability as one of the great directors of his time. But *Hell's Hinges* speaks as effectively for Hart's creative talent as anything that could be written about him. It stands as a milestone in the long history of the Western genre—a milestone in the overall vision of what a Western film can be, if the person responsible for it is as convinced as Hart was in the rightness of his approach. Hart refused to change this approach as he made film after film until 1925, when he bowed out of movie making. And the legacy he left stands up well when compared to hundreds of lesser Westerns that followed his efforts. Whatever his deficiencies, he was a giant in his field.

The Iron Horse (1924)

Filmmakers in the silent era, busy turning out cheap, action-filled cowboy thrillers and serials, attempted few first-quality Western movies. One of the few epic Westerns remembered from the silent era is John Ford's *The Iron Horse*. It was the first epic Western made by the man most film critics consider the greatest Western director of all.

Ford was a crusty New Englander of Irish descent who got an early start in the movie-making business. Cutting his teeth on short, low-budget Westerns, including some with Tom Mix, he had made nearly 40 such horse operas by the time he was 29 years old, when he directed *The Iron Horse*. He had also written many of the scripts for his films and had well-developed ideas about what makes a movie work. He had built a good reputation as a director, and the executives of Fox studios entrusted him to make this Western on a grand scale. They were encouraged by the success of another epic, *The Covered Wagon*, made by another studio a year earlier.

Ford brought personal vision and a great deal of expertise to his first spectacular film. He chose to make virtually the entire movie on location, at a time when most films were made in studios and on studio lots.

The Iron Horse is about the building of the transcontinental railroad and the famous joining of the rails at Promontory Point, Utah. Framed within this epic story, the plot had the hero searching for the murderer of his

One of the realistic outdoor sets in *The Iron Horse*. The production required 6000 extras and about 100 cooks just to feed them. William Fox intended the film to be his studio's answer to Paramount's *The Covered Wagon*, and it was an epic that ran over two hours on the screen.

father—a common Western plot device. Ford brought the whole thing off nicely with spectacular photography, thrilling action and crowd scenes. At two hours and forty minutes, *The Iron Horse* is still a long film, even by present standards. Film historians have pointed out that it contains 1280 separate scenes and 275 subtitles—a mammoth undertaking in any era.

The star of the film was George O'Brien, who went on to become one of the top Western stars in both the silent and sound film years. He had been a stunt man and an assistant cameraman on Tom Mix movies, and later directed some of his own films.

One of the chief villains was Fred Kohler, who later became one of the primary Western villains in Hollywood for many years. Jack O'Brien, George's brother, had a good part in the film, and Madge Bellamy played the heroine.

The making of such a grand-scale movie on location required tremendous logistical support. Listed in the cast were an entire regiment of US Cavalry, three thousand railroad laborers, a thousand Chinese laborers, eight hundred Indians, two thousand horses, thirteen hundred buffalo and ten thousand head of cattle.

Filming in a remote Nevada location, the movie unit had to provide food and sleeping facilities for all these people and sustenance for the livestock. The unit crews built two entire towns (which were shown in the film) along a railroad. They also provided 56 railroad coaches for transportation and even published a daily newspaper for cast and crew. There was no air conditioning, and the people involved in this movie coped with almost as many hardships as the original builders of the railroad had.

Unlike his contemporaries in the 20s, Ford made great use of moving cameras, rather than stationing them in one spot. This was very effective in the action and battle scenes. In one of the major battle scenes, Indians are charging and encircling a trapped locomotive. Ford had his cameramen shoot the action from several different angles at once, then varied these shots in the editing process to build excitement. He also interspersed scenes of the rescue party in another train engine and cavalry troops with those of the battle. This is common today, but was innovative in 1924.

Some of the dramatic camera shots Ford made in *The Iron Horse* came to typify his work in most of the films he made throughout his long career. Examples are a group of Indians on the crest of a hill, and a gang of cowboys fading into a dusty sunset. You can see similar shots in most Ford Westerns.

The subject of *The Iron Horse*—the building of the transcontinental railroad—was one which stirred national pride, the type of subject which epic movies cover best. *The Iron Horse* was a resounding success at the box office and played for a year at the Lyric Theater in New York. One critic of the time referred to it as 'an American Odyssey', a term which came to be associated with nearly all of John Ford's films throughout his career. It fits his work as the greatest of all Western directors.

33

34

THE SOUND WESTERNS

When the capability of sound was added to motion pictures, it opened the way for creative genius to flourish as it never had before. With a whole new dimension added, the art of the motion-picture maker could be complete. This was true with Western movies, of course. It's hard to imagine today a Western without the sound of horses galloping, guns firing, and heroes and villains hitting each other in fistfights. Some silent Westerns were greater than many poor-to-mediocre horse operas with sound, but the *potential* was always greater with sound.

Curiously, Hollywood did little to reach this greater potential with Westerns in the decade after sound came in. Westerns were considered a lowly art form during the 30s, undeserving of serious efforts and big budgets. The field was virtually left to low-grade 'B' Westerns and serials

Two wandering cowboys belly up to the bar in the beginning of *The Ox-Bow Incident*—Henry Fonda and Harry Morgan. Before long they will be a part of a posse bent on lynching some accused cattle rustlers. This low-budget film has taken its place as a movie classic because of its powerful indictment of man's inhumanity to man. In this case, the inhumanity was the lynching of three innocent men.

aimed at children. No pretense at art was made with these 'oaters'. They all followed the Tom Mix hero formula or the Gene Autry singing cowboy model, and they were virtually indistinguishable. But children loved them and they were dependable money makers. Many of us have fond memories of our childhood cowboy heroes, but we can't remember the plots of any of their movies in detail.

It remained for John Ford, who had been busy making other movies and hadn't directed a Western in 13 years, to show Hollywood in 1939 that first-quality 'adult' Westerns could be a high form of cinematic art and could also be popular with the public. He had proved it years earlier, in silent film days, but times had changed and now he had to prove it again. He did it by making *Stagecoach*, a film that is still regarded as one of the great Westerns.

Stagecoach (1939)

John Ford's superb film about the passengers on a stagecoach has been called the first adult Western. This claim is disputed, since there were some mature Westerns made years earlier in the silent era. But there is little doubt that *Stagecoach* started Hollywood on a new era in which the Western movie reached its zenith as cinematic art. Replacing the good-guys-versus-bad-guys plots that were universal in Westerns, *Stagecoach* showed real human beings with both good and weakness in their character.

The film is about six stagecoach passengers, the driver, a sheriff, and an outlaw who joins them on a journey. John Wayne, in his first major role in a class 'A' production, is excellent as the outlaw, the Ringo Kid, who has been framed on a murder charge and seeks the real killers. Claire Trevor plays a prostitute fleeing a town's intolerance; Thomas Mitchell is a courageous but alcoholic doctor. There is a banker who has embezzled, a mousy salesman who shows strength later, a gambler, and a pregnant woman traveling to meet her husband. Each character's personality is revealed during the journey and the ensuing action, in which the pregnant woman gives birth, the passengers are attacked by Indians, and the Ringo Kid gets revenge on his enemies.

The film was photographed in the starkly beautiful Monument Valley in Utah, later to become a frequent Ford locale, and the grandeur and beauty of the scenery and photography set standards for all Westerns to match. Indeed, the direction and the acting also set standards. Ford got excellent performances from all the actors, showing the characters' interactions and conflict in a realistic manner. The balance he achieved between character study, panoramic vistas and action scenes is one of the keys to his success in this classic film.

The Westerner (1940)

This Samuel Goldwyn film, directed by William Wyler, was an interesting sort of hybrid Western—part melodrama and part comedy. Walter Brennan won an Oscar as best supporting actor for his portrayal of Judge Roy Bean,

Some scenes from *Stagecoach* (1939), the John Ford Western classic which told of a group of assorted passengers on a stage going into Indian Territory and their varied reactions under stress.

Above : Andy Devine, the driver, and George Bancroft, the sheriff, confront the Ringo Kid (John Wayne), whose horse has died and who wants to catch a ride on the stage.

Opposite top : John Wayne on the roof during the memorable chase sequence, firing a rifle with deadly accuracy. Later he leaps forward to control the charging horses, and the stage sweeps across the sands and outruns an Indian war party.

Right : The *Stagecoach* cast. From left to right: Andy Devine, George Bancroft, John Carradine, Donald Meek, Louise Platt, Claire Trevor and John Wayne.

36

Opposite top: Gary Cooper confronts Walter Brennan in *The Westerner* (1940). Brennan played Judge Roy Bean, who ran things his own way in Langtry, Texas, and was known as 'the law west of the Pecos.' He won an Oscar for the role. Between the two—left, Paul Hurst; right, Chill Wills.

Opposite bottom: Gary Cooper at the end of a fight in *The Westerner*, a film that told the story of a dispute over land rights and the action taken by those who considered themselves in the right.

Below: Just before the lynching in *The Ox-Bow Incident* (1943), one of the innocent victims (Anthony Quinn) says his confession to a sympathetic member of the posse (Chris-Pin Martin).

which was really the leading role in the movie. Gary Cooper was the star, however, as Cole Hardin, a drifter who comes to Bean's town, Langtry, Texas in the 1880s.

Hardin is accused of horse stealing, and Judge Bean intends to hang him. But knowing of Bean's fanatic admiration for the famous stage star, Lillie Langtry (for whom Bean has named the town) and his desire to meet her, Hardin stalls by saying he knows her. He offers to introduce the judge to Lillie. Hardin and Bean come to respect each other, but Hardin is disillusioned with Bean's ruthless ways of administering the law. Hardin actually arranges for a visit by Lillie, but just before Bean is to meet her, a gunfight erupts between the two men. Bean has burned down the fields of a rancher, and Hardin has had enough. His shot mortally wounds the judge. Just before Bean dies, Lillie Langtry arrives and he meets her. She doesn't speak, remaining as remote as the portrait of her on Bean's wall, but he dies fulfilled.

Walter Brennan plays Bean to perfection as an ornery, badly-dressed, unshaven, ruthless frontier man. But while Bean is sometimes cruel in his mistaken devotion to law and order, he also shows some compassion and a touching devotion to the greatness of Lillie Langtry. As an ordinary cowboy drifter, Cooper's role was not as demanding, but he plays it competently as always. The principal emotional theme is the love-hate relationship between the two men, which is explored at length.

Director Wyler added beauty and mastery to the film with fascinating composition in his camera shots. One of them is a close-up of the wheels of a mortician's wagon rolling slowly in front of a corpse to end a death scene. Another is Cooper's lonely face staring into a ranch window, showing him as the outsider who doesn't belong.

The Westerner wasn't entirely true to historical facts, but it was an interesting, well-made film with a slightly different Western theme.

The Ox-Bow Incident (1943)

This brilliant but controversial film directed by William Wellman explores a moral issue which could be modern, but clothes it in a Western story. The theme is lynching— the forces which drive men to violence and to take the law into their own hands. It was based on a novel published in 1938 by Walter Van Tilburg Clark, who wanted to make the point that the mob violence seen in the rise of the Nazis in Europe could occur in other places, too. By setting his story in Nevada in 1885, he hoped the Western flavor would make his message entertaining so it would reach more people.

Cowboys Gil Carter (played by Henry Fonda) and Art Croft (Harry Morgan) ride into a Nevada frontier town. The sheriff is out of town; the townspeople believe a local rancher has been murdered by cattle thieves. A vigilante group forms to hunt the criminals. They encounter three strangers—Donald Martin (played by Dana Andrews), a Mexican, and an old man—who say they have bought some cattle from the rancher. When they can't show a bill of sale, the vigilantes put them on trial as rustlers. The outsiders, Carter and Croft, argue that the trio should be brought back to town to await the sheriff's return, but the mob is out for blood. The vigilantes sentence the trio to die and allow Martin to write a farewell letter to his wife; then they are hanged. The sheriff returns the next day and tells the stunned townspeople that the rancher is alive and did sell the cattle to the hanged men. Carter reads aloud an excerpt from Martin's letter in the hushed saloon where the remorseful people gather. Then he and Croft ride out of town.

It is a powerful film with a strong message, made all the more effective by the quiet way in which it tells its story. Fonda, Andrews and the rest of the cast give solid performances. Most of the film was shot at the studio rather than on location—an unusual approach for a quality Western. It gave the film a brooding quality in keeping with its somber theme; most of the scenes are night scenes.

The message of *The Ox-Bow Incident* is that anyone could be mistaken for a criminal if punishment is handed out on impulse. The theme is still valid today.

Duel in the Sun (1946)

This lengthy color film is as filled with passion as an Italian opera, which its plot resembles. Directed by King Vidor for David O Selznick, the film's earthy, lustful quality was considered quite daring for its time and unusual for a Western.

Jennifer Jones plays Pearl, a half-breed who works for the influential Senator McCanles and his family at their ranch. Joseph Cotten plays the good son, Jesse, a reasonable man who gets romantically involved with Pearl. Gregory Peck, in a rare role as a villain, gives a strong performance as Lewt, the son who goes bad and becomes a killer. He, too, romances Pearl, becoming sexually involved with her after scenes in which they stare at each other with hot-eyed lust. Lewt refuses to marry her, so she gets engaged to another man. Lewt kills the other man, then shoots his good brother as well. Pearl tracks Lewt into the desert for revenge and they shoot it out. Both are killed.

Overshadowed by this passion is another theme—that of a struggle between ranchers and railroaders who want to run tracks across the range. It is the theme of the passing of the Old West, of cattlemen facing the reality that the wilderness cannot remain as wilderness forever in the face of progress. This theme has been treated many times since *Duel in the Sun* was made, but it was not a cliché at the time. The film might have been more effective if this theme had been less subordinated to the passion theme than it was. Nevertheless, it is an interesting story of love and violence.

The photography makes *Duel in the Sun* a very attractive movie. Great care was taken with composition, lighting and camera angles. Particularly striking are the scenes at the end, in the brilliant, scorching sun of the desert, when Lewt and Pearl meet their mutual death.

Above: Gregory Peck and Jennifer Jones in a romantic interlude before they shoot at each other in *Duel in the Sun* (1946).

Top: The lynching scene from *The Ox-Bow Incident* (1943). Marc Lawrence is about to put the noose around the neck of the first innocent victim (Dana Andrews). After the men are hanged, the sheriff arrives with the news that they were innocent and had paid for the cattle.

Top and *above :* John Wayne and Montgomery Clift in *Red River* (1948), one of the great Westerns and among the finest accomplishments of Director Howard Hawks. The love-hate battles of the two stars, as father and surrogate son, told in the context of the first cattle drive on the Chisholm Trail, gave the movie its interesting blend of character conflict and epic sweep.

The cast of *Duel in the Sun* is rounded out with some fine character actors: Charles Bickford, Walter Huston, Lionel Barrymore, Lillian Gish, and old-time Western star Harry Carey. The film may not be one of the greatest Westerns, but its visual beauty is memorable.

Red River (1948)

This big, epic film about cattle drives is a favorite of many fans. It gave John Wayne the chance to play the most complex good/bad man role he had experienced until that time. And it marked the screen debut of Montgomery Clift, a brilliant actor from Broadway who had never acted in a Western drama. Doubt existed that two such dissimilar actors as Wayne and Clift could play effectively against each other, but the results proved otherwise. They were excellent together.

Red River was also the first Western that Howard Hawks directed in his impressive Hollywood career. John Ireland, Joanne Dru, Walter Brennan, Colleen Gray and Shelley Winters had supporting parts.

The story is about Tom Dunson, a bitter, aging cattle rancher (played by Wayne) whose fiancee has been killed by Indians. He rescues a boy, Matt (played by Clift when he reaches adulthood), from the attack and raises him as a foster son. Dunson has such a rigid code of morals and dictatorial ways that Matt becomes alienated as he learns the cattle business from him. The story is about a huge cattle herd that Dunson must drive to a railway point for shipment to market. He wants to take a dangerous route to Abilene, but Matt insists they should take a safer route to Kansas City. They fight over this. Later, when Dunson kills one of the cowhands, Matt and other cowboys take over the herd and head for Kansas City. Along the way, Matt meets and falls in love with Tess (Joanne Dru). When Dunson catches up with Matt, they have a vicious fight, taking out all their father/son resentment on each other. But Tess brings them to their senses, stopping the fight with a rifle and reasoning. Throughout the film realistic details of the work involved in a huge cattle drive are presented. The viewer feels as though he were there on the dusty plains.

With exterior scenes photographed in a remote part of Arizona, the film required nine thousand head of cattle and five hundred actors to accomplish Hawks' goal of a big, wide, spectacular movie showing the grandeur of the West. He succeeded in making a very good, realistic Western with fine characterization and a solid story. Over the years, it has earned recognition as a true Western classic.

The Gunfighter (1950)

This tense, somber Western is about the passing of the Old West—not, as in other films, the surrender of cattle range-land to progress, but the changing of moral codes which make the gunfighter an out-of-date relic of the past. *The Gunfighter* doesn't feature cattle drives or hard-riding

posses chasing villains in wide vistas. Virtually the entire story takes place in a town—a drab, realistic town inhabited by plain, hard-working people in drab clothes.

Gregory Peck, changed in appearance with a drooping moustache, plays an aging gunfighter, Johnny Ringo, who comes to town and visits the sheriff, an old friend. The rest of the townspeople want nothing to do with him, because of his reputation as a killer—'the top gun in the West.' Ringo would like to settle down, find another occupation, because he knows that gunfighters are becoming out of date and he's tired of the life. But he is constantly haunted and challenged by younger gunmen who would love to gain fame by killing the old 'top gun.' Ringo refuses to leave town despite the hostility; it appears he is waiting to decide his fate. The tension constantly builds as the old gunfighter's quest for peace is stymied. He must live with his legend, even though the real man is not the legend any longer. The day of reckoning comes when a young punk gunfighter proves faster than Ringo and kills him. The swaggering victor is told that sooner or later, he will meet someone who is faster with a gun than he is; he is doomed to be shot some day.

The essential message of *The Gunfighter* is that the only retirement home for gunfighters is the cemetery. It is a sad story with a downbeat ending. It is the exact opposite of the glorification of gunfighting that is common in many Westerns. But it is also a good story, beautifully paced, with excellent acting in a low-key manner by Peck. Richard

Above left : Gregory Peck is shot in *The Gunfighter* (1950). Jean Parker is at the left. The role as a gunman who is a real person with human emotions had originally been asked for by John Wayne.

Above right : In *The Gunfighter* Peck played a gunslinger named Johnny Ringo. His performance in this film has been called one of his best.

Opposite top : In the classic, *High Noon* (1952), Gary Cooper marries Grace Kelly, who played the part of an innocent Quaker woman who hated violence of any kind.

Opposite bottom : High Noon tells the story of one man, Marshal Will Kane (Gary Cooper, here with Katy Jurado) and his search for support against a gang of revengeful outlaws. He can find no help and takes on the gang single-handedly.

Jaeckel, as the young gunman who kills Ringo, and Millard Mitchell, as the sheriff, are very effective.

Director Henry King fashioned a fine movie, shooting it on the back lot at Twentieth Century-Fox except for one day's location shooting. The critics praised the film, but fans of Gregory Peck, the movie's drawing card, complained about his moustache. *The Gunfighter* stands as one of the best Westerns of the 50s.

High Noon (1952)

High Noon is generally regarded as one of the great, classic Westerns of all time. It was regarded as a classic from the day of its release and its reputation has held up well since then. The moral theme of its story applies to society today as well as to the nineteenth century West; it just happened that the story was told in a Western. The message is about the need for citizens of a democratic community to take responsibility for upholding the community's laws. It is also about a man taking a moral stand based on his principles and adhering to that stand despite the odds against him.

In *High Noon*, Marshal Will Kane (Gary Cooper) marries a Quaker woman (Grace Kelly) who is, naturally, a pacifist. He soon learns that a killer he helped convict and send to jail has been released and is returning to the town with three outlaw companions for revenge against the marshal. Kane's wife declares she will leave on the noon

Some scenes from *Shane* (1953).

Top: Alan Ladd, as Shane, who is a sort of avenging archangel drifter, is hired by Heflin as a farm worker, but he later turns out to be a gunfighter with a heart of gold.

Opposite top: Van Heflin, the homesteader, presides at the funeral of another homesteader (Elisha Cook, Jr), who has been killed in an unfair gunfight with Jack Palance, a hired killer. Palance's bullet had caused Cook to fly several feet backward on impact, probably the most realistic shooting filmed up to the time the picture was made.

Opposite bottom: Heflin, after talking the other homesteaders into staying on their property, decides to ride into town to face down the villain. Here he loads his gun while his wife, Jean Arthur, looks on.

train with or without him, but Kane knows he must remain to do his duty and fight the men. When he tries to enlist support for a force of law and order, the townspeople will not help him. Even his deputy refuses, telling him it is hopeless to resist the outlaws. His wife boards the noon train and the outlaw gang arrives. In a running gun battle, Kane manages to kill three of the outlaws. With the situation desperate, his wife kills the fourth. Then, with a look of disgust, Kane throws his badge on the ground and boards the train with his wife, leaving the cowardly townspeople forever.

Gary Cooper won an Academy Award for his superb portrayal of the beleaguered marshal. Cooper played him not as a dauntless Western super hero, but as a tired, fearful man with pain in his eyes and anxiety on his face. He knows his chances alone against the outlaws are slim; he doesn't want to die; but he is morally bound to do his duty. Grace Kelly was perfect as the pure, pacifist wife. Lloyd Bridges, Thomas Mitchell, Katy Jurado and the rest of the supporting cast was excellent.

The movie is about eighty-five minutes in Kane's life, reflecting real time, minute for minute, with the ticking of the town clock measuring it. The suspense in this taut, realistic film held audiences spellbound until the end. Director Fred Zinnemann created a rare and brilliant movie, worthy of the label 'classic.'

Shane (1953)

It is interesting to note that in the long history of Western movie making, two of the finest Westerns of all time, *High Noon* and *Shane*, were made within a year of one another. The two films took different approaches. *High Noon* was a tight, eighty-five minute story in black and white, filmed on a studio lot. *Shane* was a big, spectacular color film, thirty-three minutes longer than *High Noon* and shot on location.

Producer/director George Stevens spent $3 million to make *Shane* in the colorful Jackson Hole country in Wyoming. His strikingly beautiful photography made it one of the handsomest movies of any ty . ever filmed. But other Westerns have been just as spectacu!: and expensive to make without attaining the greatness of *Shane*.

Part of the answer lies in the plot and the personal vision of the director, who had a firm idea of what this movie should be. It is a simple story with a deliberate pace about the dying of the Old West with its gunslingers and its cattle barons in the face of settlers and the civilizing influence of law. This is not an original theme for Westerns; other good movies had addressed it before. But the way in which Stevens tells his story, with tremendous attention to details and care for beautiful photography and mood, makes it more effective than others. He tells it in the personal stories of well-developed characters, set against the larger panorama of the changing West.

Shane, a gunfighter (played by Alan Ladd), arrives at the isolated farm of a settler (Van Heflin) a few miles from a

45

small Wyoming town. Shane is trying to forget his violent past and find work as a farm hand, knowing that the days of gunfighters are just about over. The settler, named Starrett, gives the taciturn stranger a job and a place to sleep in the barn. Starret's wife and young son, Joey (played by Jean Arthur and Brandon de Wilde, respectively), excited by the presence of a stranger in their drab, isolated farm lives, take a liking to Shane immediately. Joey develops a kind of hero worship when Shane quietly shows him how to use a gun and displays his own prowess.

Trouble comes when a cattle baron named Ryker burns some neighboring settlers' farms and threatens to drive all the farmers in the area out unless they sell him their land. Starrett, a decent, stubborn man, angrily refuses to sell and Ryker hires a top-flight gunslinger named Wilson (Jack Palance) to intimidate the settlers. Shane wants no part of the violence building up, since he doesn't want to go back to gunfighting, even though he is taunted by Ryker's bullying employees. After Wilson brutally shoots down a settler, farmer Starrett intends to have a showdown with Ryker. But he is waylaid by Shane, who has had enough and straps on his gun. He shoots it out with Wilson in a classic gunfighters' duel and then shoots Ryker and his men, ending the threat to the settlers. Now that he has revealed himself as a deadly gunfighter, Shane realizes he has no place with the settlers and rides off, leaving young Joey pleading, 'Come back, Shane!'

Stevens constructed a ramshackle Western town and the Starrett home on location in Wyoming. He insisted on absolute authenticity in clothing, buildings, tools and scenery—everything in the film, whether the audience noticed it or not. He continued shooting each outdoor scene when clouds passed overhead, where most directors would pause. This gave the film a moody realism. He also wanted a muddy main street in the little town and poured water over the dirt to make it that way, so that the actors' boots sank in the mud. To show the impact of a bullet striking a man, he attached a wire to each actor playing a victim and had the wire yanked as the shot was fired, thus jerking the victim backward.

All this care by a perfectionist resulted in an extraordinary Western. Stevens also coaxed excellent performances from his cast. Alan Ladd gave the best performance of his life as Shane and Jack Palance won an Oscar nomination for his. Cinematographer Loyal Griggs won an Academy Award for his color photography.

Shane may have covered familiar story material, but the way in which Stevens made his film transformed it into one of the great Western classics.

The Man From Laramie (1955)

This was one of several first-quality Western productions in which James Stewart starred in the fifties. Stewart, of course, is one of the giants of the film industry and didn't specialize in Westerns. But when he did appear in them, he proved he could hold his own with the Western stars.

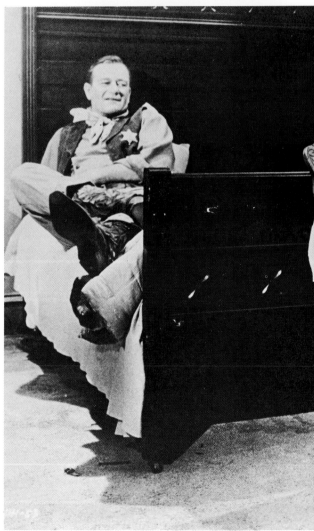

Above : Stewart gets into trouble in *The Man From Laramie*. In the 1950s, Western film roles enabled him to age and still retain his position in as a soft-spoken hero.

Opposite top : James Stewart in *The Man From Laramie* (1955), a taut action tale of revenge, with Stewart seeking those who killed his brother.

Below : Dean Martin gets a shave from Angie Dickinson, as John Wayne looks on in *Rio Bravo* (1959). It was the story of a sheriff (Wayne) and his relationships with a former deputy (Martin) who had become a worthless drunk over a woman, and reclaims himself during the moment of crisis when Wayne is confronted by a town tough and his family.

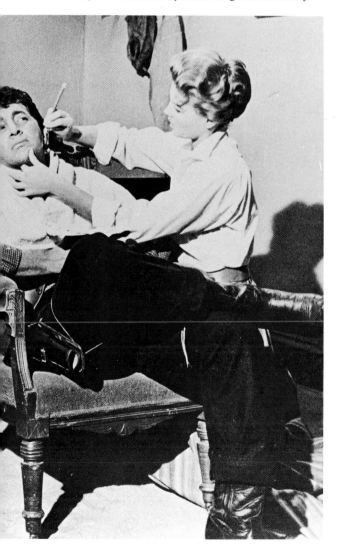

The Man From Laramie is a good example of the psychologically motivated, action-packed Westerns that were popular in the 50s. Stewart plays Will Lockhart, an army officer in civilian disguise who is trying to find out who sold some rifles to the Apaches. He has a burning motivation: the Indians had killed his brother in an ambush using the weapons. His search takes him to a wealthy, influential rancher, Alec Waggoman (Donald Crisp), who is old and going blind. The old rancher is an arrogant but basically decent man who loves his worthless, immature son, Dave, and wants him to take over the ranch when he dies. Lockhart becomes embroiled in fights with Dave (played by Alex Nicol) and the ranch foreman, (Arthur Kennedy) in his search. It turns out that Dave and the foreman sold the rifles to the Apaches, a fact which tortures old Alec, who has nightmares about a man coming to kill his son. The foreman kills Dave in a fight, the Indians kill the foreman, and the old man finds his relief from sorrow in his own death. Only then does Lockhart's obsession end.

Director Anthony Mann added quality to this ordinary plot by his impressive photography of landscapes, which lent itself well to wide-screen Cinemascope, in which this film was made. It was shot on location in more than a dozen settings near Santa Fe, New Mexico. The interaction between the characters is one of the movie's strong points, showing the audience the inner torments that these people suffered.

Stewart gives a fine, laconic performance, his essential decency having strong appeal. Donald Crisp is very good as the old rancher, and the rest of the cast is first-rate. *The Man From Laramie* is not one of the great Westerns, but it represents the high standards met in the 50s.

Rio Bravo (1959)

The origin of this movie is interesting. Howard Hawks, one of Hollywood's leading directors, didn't like the theme of the classic *High Noon*, filmed by Fred Zinnemann several years earlier. He didn't believe the citizens of any 19th-century Western town would refuse to help the sheriff protect the town, as they did to Gary Cooper in that film. When asked to make a Western the way he thought it should be done, he came up with *Rio Bravo*. It turned out to be a very good film.

In this story, the sheriff or marshal of Tucson, Arizona, played by John Wayne, is threatened with attack by a gang of outlaws after jailing one of them. Wayne is prepared to fight them alone, but many townspeople offer to help him. Even Dude, his former deputy (played by Dean Martin), who has been on a two-year drinking bender, sobers up to help him. Another volunteer is an irascible old cripple (Walter Brennan). There is also a young gunslinger (Ricky Nelson) who is at first reluctant to get involved but does join the marshal. The outlaws kidnap Dude and offer to exchange him for their jailed comrade, but Wayne and his helpers use guns and dynamite to rout the gang.

Besides taking the opposite tack of *High Noon* and still

Some scenes from *Ride the High Country* (1962).

Top : The wedding scene in which Mariette Hartley is wed to a miner who turns out to be a heel. She realizes her mistake and escapes the mining camp with Joel McCrae and Randolph Scott, who play the parts of two old-time lawmen who had signed on to escort gold from the goldfields to the bank.

Opposite top : Randolph Scott, left, and Joel McCrae, in their last performances as Western heroes, were given the best roles of their lives, and they made the most of it. It was a controlled, subtle film and was directed by Sam Peckinpah.

Opposite bottom : Joel McCrae (left) and Mariette Hartley (center) are ready for the attack by Mariette's rotter of a husband and his gang.

being a good movie, *Rio Bravo* was a turning point for John Wayne, who was established as the top Western star already, but who had played serious characters. *Rio Bravo*'s long story is filled with humor, and Wayne's character is gruff, tough, but also humorous. For the rest of his career, Wayne played characters with humorous aspects in most of his films.

The choice of Dean Martin to play opposite Wayne seemed unlikely, but he gave a very good performance as the comic drunk and interacted well with Wayne. Ricky Nelson, another unlikely choice, was effective as the young gunfighter. Walter Brennan gave his usual solid performance as the ornery oldtimer, and Angie Dickinson provided the love interest for Wayne.

Rio Bravo marked a turning away from psychological Westerns in the 50s; it was aimed purely at entertainment. The director and cast made it so entertaining that it has joined the list of Westerns aficionados call classics.

Ride the High Country (1962)

This low-budget color movie was released as a sort of 'B' Western to play on double bills at drive-in theaters. But director Sam Peckinpah and stars Randolph Scott and Joel McCrea surprised MGM by making such a natural and appealing film that it won awards in Europe, made money, and came to be regarded as one of the great Westerns.

Old friends Scott and McCrea thought of this as their last movie before retirement. It was for Scott, but McCrea changed his mind later and did a couple more films. Both had enjoyed long careers, neither specializing in Westerns exclusively. But each had worked his way through countless 'B' Westerns and looked more natural on a horse than most other actors. They both considered *Ride the High Country* as a sort of final chapter of Western movies, depicting the demise of the Old West.

McCrea played an old-time cowboy, Steve Judd, who is hired to transport a load of gold from a mining camp to town. He hires an old friend, Gil Westrum (Scott) and his young pal, Heck Longtree (Ron Starr) to help him guard the gold during the journey. Considering it the chance of a lifetime, Westrum tries to persuade Judd to steal the gold and split it three ways, but Judd refuses. They pick up a companion, Elsa (Mariette Hartley), and attend her wild and bawdy wedding and reception (in a bordello) to a ruffian. She flees the wedding party with them, with her bridegroom's wild family in hot pursuit. Westrum and Longtree attempt to steal the gold, but Judd catches them and swears he will bring them in for trial. During the long chase by her in-laws, Elsa falls in love with Longtree. A showdown with the in-laws is coming, but Judd and Westrum split and Westrum rides off. When he hears the shooting start, though, he comes back to help his old friend. Judd is mortally wounded in their victory over the in-laws. In a touching, underplayed scene, the two old friends say farewell and Westrum promises to bring the gold to town. They both know this is the end for their kind of Westerner and their way of life.

Everything about *Ride the High Country* has the ring of truth—the unglamorized setting, the dialogue and the natural acting. It's a natural Western, and a very good one.

For a Few Dollars More (1965)

This was probably the best of the so-called 'Spaghetti Westerns' that proliferated in Europe in the 60s and early 70s. It was the second in a trilogy made by Italian director Sergio Leone starring Clint Eastwood. The first was *A Fistful of Dollars* and the third was *The Good, The Bad, and The Ugly*.

The 'Spaghetti Western' was and is controversial, but there is no doubt that it provided an interesting and different approach to the Western genre. It was a European vision of the American West, with a touch of grim humor, gratuitous violence, weird-looking characters and strange, jarring soundtrack music. Almost an abstract parody of the typical Western. But American audiences liked these violent, action-packed films while they were in vogue.

In *For a Few Dollars More*, Clint Eastwood plays a totally ruthless sort of anti-hero—an unkempt, unshaven bounty hunter known simply as 'The Man With No Name'. He rides into town, corners his wanted man in a saloon and kills him. Then he meets another bounty hunter, Colonel Mortimer (played by Lee Van Cleef) and they work together. The Man With No Name infiltrates the gang of a notorious outlaw named Indio, who killed the Colonel's sister years earlier. The plan is to get Indio and his gang and split the reward. Later, the gang finds out that The Man With No Name is an infiltrator and Mortimer comes to help him. The unnamed bounty hunter saves the Colonel's life by preventing Indio from shooting him. After a violent gun battle, the only outlaw left alive is Indio. At this point, The Man With No Name referees a classic gun duel between Mortimer and Indio. The Colonel wins and avenges his sister's murder, then gives his share of the bounty money to his partner.

Clint Eastwood, who had not reached stardom after a decade in Hollywood, got his big break in these Sergio Leone movies. His hard, squint-eyed characters became his model for stardom. Van Cleef, too, became one of the most popular actors in Europe after years of playing villains in US films. *For a Few Dollars More* has a strange aura, but it is an immensely interesting film, an example of a fresh approach to the Western.

True Grit (1969)

This big, beautifully photographed color film managed to put a fresh face on a typical Western story because of the zest with which it was directed and acted. It combines comedy, sentiment and action in a winning formula. Directed by the veteran Henry Hathaway, it resulted in an Academy Award for John Wayne, capping his legendary acting career.

50

Above : Clint Eastwood as the stranger in *For a Few Dollars More* (1965), strolls into a Mexican cantina. This film was a spaghetti Western sequel to *A Fistful of Dollars* (1964), and tells the story of a man with no name, a bounty hunter, and is filled with violence as he and his partner search for Mexican bandits.

Left : Wayne won an Oscar for his role as Rooster Cogburn in *True Grit*. In the picture, Cogburn, an over-the-hill, one-eyed, crotchety US marshal, helps a 14-year-old girl (Darby) track down her father's killer.

Opposite top : In *The Good, the Bad and the Ugly* (1966), Eastwood is still playing the violent man with no name. Here he encourages one of his enemies to hang himself.

Opposite bottom : John Wayne and Kim Darby in *True Grit* (1969).

Wayne played Rooster Cogburn, a gruff, ornery former lawman with one eye and a spreading midsection, but who also has 'true grit'—the courage to do what's right, despite the odds. The father of a teenage girl named Mattie Ross (Kim Darby) has been killed by a man named Tom Chaney. Mattie offers Rooster Cogburn $50 to capture Chaney so he will be punished. She also talks a Texas Ranger named Le Boeuf (Glen Campbell) into helping. Mattie insists on going with the men, although they protest. When they find out that Chaney has joined a gang of outlaws headed by Ned Pepper (Robert Duvall), they unsuccessfully attack the outlaws. Mattie is captured by Chaney and held hostage, forcing Rooster and Le Boeuf to ride away. But in the climactic scene, the old lawman returns and charges at the gang on horseback, yelling 'Fill your hands, you sons of bitches!' He wipes out the gang and Chaney is brought to justice. Le Boeuf is killed in the fight, and Mattie bids goodbye to Rooster as he rides away.

This story of an aging lawman is about growing old, about dying, and about his reflections and regrets on his past life. In his relationship with the teenager, Wayne effectively combines gruffness and a touching sentimentality as he tells her of his life, his broken marriage and his need for independence. But the story also has broad comedy by Wayne and others, and a lot of well-staged action. The scene of old Rooster defeating the outlaw gang is not really believable, but somehow it doesn't matter in this tale and it made the audiences cheer.

There's nothing subtle about *True Grit*; the good guys are all honest and the villains are evil through and through. But it's an entertaining mix of funny, sad, tender and thrilling action that adds up to a good Western.

Butch Cassidy and the Sundance Kid (1969)

Charm is the greatest factor in the success of this superb Western. The story of the last of the famous Western outlaws is told with warmth, comedy, romance and nostalgia, while at the same time being true to the lives of its subjects. George Roy Hill's marvelous direction and beautiful photography makes this one of the most pleasing Westerns ever filmed.

History notes that Butch Cassidy, the Sundance Kid and their gang of bank and train robbers were fun-loving types who managed to avoid killing people while committing their crimes. This is the way Paul Newman and Robert Redford play Butch and Sundance in the film, and their talents and relationship on screen are perfect. A pretty schoolteacher, Etta Place (Katharine Ross), is looking for adventure and joins the two outlaws. She helps them set up bank robberies by scouting the banks. But Butch and Sundance are so successful that their reputation grows, putting pressure on law officials to catch them. The famed Pinkerton men pursue them relentlessly, causing Cassidy to ask repeatedly, 'Who *are* those guys?'

The film switches frequently from comic adventures to exciting action to romance. The romance is provided when

Above : John Wayne at the end of the magnificent final gunfight in *True Grit*. The box office take on this film was the highest ever recorded by a John Wayne picture—$14,250,000—and it was a well-deserved profit.

Opposite top : Paul Newman (left) starred with Robert Redford and Katharine Ross in *Butch Cassidy and the Sundance Kid* (1969). The film was based upon the lives of two legendary bank- and train-robbers who clowned their way through much of the 1890s before fleeing to South America.

Opposite bottom : One of the train robberies in *Butch Cassidy and the Sundance Kid*. The tension and suspense of the film are embodied in the pursuit of the two by a persistent posse.

Etta and the Sundance Kid fall in love, with lush photography and romantic soundtrack music setting the mood. Etta gets tired of running all the time, so the three of them move to South America to start a new life. Butch and Sundance change their names and work in a mining camp, but life is too dull and soon they begin their robberies again. Etta decides to return to the United States. By now the Pinkertons have located the two men and they engage the help of the local militia to shoot them down. Trapped, Butch and Sundance make a last stand and charge into a hail of bullets. The film freezes at this point, instead of showing them bleeding and dead like the outlaws in *Bonnie and Clyde*. They are such sympathetic characters that the audience is spared the agony of seeing them die.

The acting of Newman, Redford and the rest of the cast is first-rate, matching the fine direction. The tone of the film is one of fun, rather than realism, but that is the heart of its charm and entertainment value.

Little Big Man (1970)

The number of Western films, particularly good ones, dwindled to very few in the decade of the 70s. Many film critics consider the best Western of that period to be *Little Big Man*, directed by Arthur Penn and starring Dustin Hoffman and Dan George, a Canadian Indian.

Opposite top : Dustin Hoffman, in *Little Big Man* (1970), played the part of Jack Crabb, a white who was captured by the Indians as a boy and took on their way of life.

Opposite bottom : Director Arthur Penn used panoramic outdoor scenes in *Little Big Man*.

Below : Paul Newman and Katharine Ross in their famous light-hearted bicycle-riding scene to the tune of 'Raindrops Keep Falling on my Head' in *Butch Cassidy and the Sundance Kid*.

The film is about the adventures of Jack Crabb, a 120-year-old man who says he is the sole white survivor of the battle of the Little Big Horn. It is a remarkable review of the history of the West in modern terms, told by this eyewitness. At first, the witness is a ten-year-old boy, raised by the Cheyenne Indians after his parents are killed by other Indians. Trapped by two cultures, he struggles to determine who and what he is. He is rescued by whites after five years and lives in that culture with disastrous results. He experiences two marriages, bankruptcy and alcoholism, risking death from both whites and Indians at various times. He finally finds himself on the battlefield, fighting the Indians with Custer in Custer's last stand. He is saved by an old friend and thus he is the only white man who survives that battle. The film is alternately comic, touching and bitter. Its violent scenes of massacres of Indian women, men and children are designed to be vivid reminders of man's capability of cruelty.

The film is based on historical research, although told through the eyes of an imaginary witness. It is also Arthur Penn's personal vision of the West's history, reflecting his attitudes. Custer is portrayed as a cruel, arrogant, pompous fool, with no pity given. The film is a clear-eyed reevaluation of some of the romanticized myths of the West, stripping away the myths and replacing them with gritty, vivid reality.

Dan George is very impressive as Old Lodge Skins, the Cheyenne chief. He embodies the dignity, pride and endurance of his people, at last giving the Indian his due on film. Dustin Hoffman is similarly impressive, with the help of remarkable makeup jobs to show him aging. He gives his usual outstanding performance, and this mixture of comedy and tragedy is a milestone in Western movies. It is a real work of art, dedicated to the cause of peace and the brotherhood of man.

Rooster Cogburn (1975)

The immense appeal of John Wayne's characterization of Rooster Cogburn in *True Grit* six years earlier spawned the idea for this sequel. Wayne's crusty, hard-drinking old marshal needed an appealing character to play against, and it was decided that Katharine Hepburn would be the perfect partner. It was an inspired pairing; these two aging Hollywood legends, who had never appeared together in a film before, lit up the screen with the interplay of their powerful personalities. As a result, the film is a triumph of personality and performance over a thin plot.

Old Cogburn, constantly criticized by the district judge (John McIntyre), is stripped of his badge and forced to retire with his Chinese cook and a cat who drinks liquor. When a vicious young killer named Hawk (Richard Jordan) kills a US Cavalry escort and steals a wagonload of nitroglycerin, Cogburn is asked to come out of retirement to pursue him. The old marshal meets Eula Goodnight (Hepburn), a spinster whose religious mission has been destroyed by Hawk. She insists on accompanying Cogburn

Opposite top : The Battle of the Little Big Horn, as staged by Director Arthur Penn in *Little Big Man.*

Opposite bottom : After *True Grit*, John Wayne reappeared in a re-creation of his role in another film, *Rooster Cogburn* (1975), co-starring with Katharine Hepburn.

Below : Makeup man Dick Smith created this makeup for Dustin Hoffman showing Jack Crabb at the age of 121, retelling the story of his life in *Little Big Man*. Crabb, an Army scout, claimed to be the sole survivor of Custer's last stand at the Little Big Horn.

in his pursuit of Hawk. The feisty, high-minded woman collides with the gruff, hard-drinking marshal throughout their journey, setting the perfect stage for Hepburn and Wayne to engage their forceful talents. Along the way, she tries to reform him, he resists and growls at her, and they learn to respect each other. The respect turns into affection and love by the end of the film.

Cogburn, of course, apprehends the outlaws and justice prevails in the end. But this is nearly incidental to the main force of the movie, which explores the relationship between the marshal and the Bible-toting spinster. The powerful talents of the two stars, engaging in humor and tenderness, are so dominating that audiences hardly noticed that the movie had little in the way of a plot.

Director Stuart Millar did a fine job of photographing the beautiful Oregon scenery on location, and the film has great visual appeal. With this and the compelling performances of two Hollywood legends, *Rooster Cogburn* was a box office hit, and it hardly mattered that it is not a great Western.

The Shootist (1976)

John Wayne's last feature-length film could be interpreted as a final eulogy capping his long career, and perhaps he had that in mind when he accepted his role. Wayne plays the last of a dying breed of gunfighter, a legend who has outlived his time. It is 1901 and this 'shootist,' as he is called, rides into Carson City to visit a doctor who is an old friend. The doctor, played by James Stewart, examines his ailing friend and gives him the terrible news: he is dying of cancer and has only a short time to live. To the old shootist, J B Books, this seems fitting because he already knows that with the automobile and electricity ushering in a new age, his time is up. There is no place in the new age for old gunfighters.

This moving, sensitive Western is about the last eight

days in the life of Books. He wants a quiet death, but his celebrity makes this impossible. The widow who runs the boarding house where he stays (Lauren Bacall) wants to evict him because of the hero worship her young son (Ron Howard) has for him. The barber saves clippings from the gunman's hair to sell for souvenirs and the undertaker plans to exhibit his corpse and charge admission. In addition, some shady characters (Richard Boone and Hugh O'Brien) would love to gun down the enfeebled legend and make their own reputations.

Books tries to make the worshipping son of the landlady understand that his own moral code, which has served him well while killing 30 men in his long career, must be changed to suit a changing world. The landlady, too, becomes deeply fond of the dying gunman as she gets to know him. But the burden of his legend threatens him at every turn, and he decides to hasten his death by taking on the shady characters in one last gunfight. It happens in a saloon, in the best tradition of Western films, and the old gunfighter manages to kill his adversaries in one last burst of skill and courage. But he, too, is fatally wounded, ending his life as he wishes it to end.

Don Siegel directed the film with eloquent restraint. It could have been played for sentimentality all the way, but instead it is presented in a clear-eyed, unsentimental manner, true to the John Wayne tradition. The low-keyed approach makes use of fine photography and a first-rate supporting cast worthy of Wayne's finale.

The Outlaw Josey Wales (1976)

This film was made after Clint Eastwood had emerged from his 'Spaghetti Western' phase and had reached superstardom with American audiences. It uses the well-worn 'revenge' plot and features plenty of outdoor action, hard riding and gunfights. Still, Eastwood makes it work well by the magnetism of his personal popularity and his ease in the Western genre. Eastwood also directed the film, set in the Civil War period.

The story opens with Eastwood as a farmer in Missouri, plowing his fields. A band of Union sympathizers similar to Quantrill's raiders burns down his house, raping and kidnapping his wife and killing his young son. Bent on revenge, he joins a band of southern sympathizers to fight the enemy raiders. Tricked into a trap, all but Eastwood surrender and are treacherously murdered. He is hunted all over Missouri and Kansas; he takes refuge with an Indian nation. There he is befriended by an old Indian (Chief Dan George). Eastwood later heads west through Kansas and rescues the mother and daughter of a Kansas man who fought against his band of southern sympathizers. He has a romance with the daughter (Sondra Locke) and eventually finds and kills the leaders of the band who burned his home. The old Indian friend helps him all the way.

Although the plot is trite, Eastwood makes the film exciting with his well-staged action scenes. The photography of wide outdoor scenes is in the tradition of good

Western films. There is nothing innovative about this film, but it is a good representation of the mainstream tradition of the Western genre.

Above: A scene from *Tom Horn* (1979). Steve McQueen as Tom Horn, a bounty hunter and, according to Warner Brothers, 'one of the last great heroes of the American West,' shares a tender moment with Linda Evans, who played a school-teacher in the outdoor adventure-drama. The studio used a slogan for the picture—'See him before he sees you.'

Tom Horn (1980)

This is one of the last two films Steve McQueen made shortly before his death. McQueen reportedly became interested in a film on Tom Horn because of his interest in Western history. Horn was a real person—one of the last of the hired gunmen in the West. At the turn of the century, when most other gunmen were dead or retired, Horn was still working for cattlemen and other business-men killing rustlers. But he, too, outlived his time and met a tragic end.

The film, directed by William Wiard, is about Tom Horn's last days in a raw Wyoming town. The new breed of men who run such towns is made up of businessmen who set up chambers of commerce, subdivide rangeland and sell it. They have hired Horn to wipe out a menacing gang of rustlers because of his reputation as a fearless and ruthless gunman who kills for pay. Horn does his job with his usual efficiency, but his killing skills and his cantankerous inde-pendence make the businessmen afraid that they won't be able to make him do what they want in the future. He is regarded as a danger to them, so they frame him for the murder of a teenage boy. They know just how to set the

Opposite: Klinton Spilsbury starred in the title role in *The Legend of the Lone Ranger* (1981).

machinery of the law in motion, with the cooperation of the sheriff, and they succeed in jailing Horn. The film takes its time in showing how hopeless is Horn's fight to prove his innocence. It also moves at a deliberate pace in showing his execution, his cool courage and the mixed emotions of his executioners.

McQueen gives a moving and believable performance as the gunman who becomes resigned to his fate. His weather-beaten features and his quiet underplaying of the role are very effective in an emotional story.

Director Wiard does a fine job of fashioning a good, solid Western with a tragic message. The film is a good Western in a time when few films of this genre are being made.

The Legend of The Lone Ranger (1981)

The Lone Ranger certainly must be considered one of the great fictional heroes of the West. For nearly half a century, youngsters have grown up familiar with his cry of 'Hi-yo Silver!' and the strains of the William Tell overture. In comic books, on radio and television, and in movie serials of the 30s and 40s, the 'daring and resourceful masked rider of the plains' thrilled countless millions of youngsters. Brace Beemer (on radio), Clayton Moore (on television) and a number of other actors have played the Ranger over the years.

This film, directed by William A Fraker, was the first attempt in some years to exploit the Lone Ranger legend in a full-length movie. It purports to tell the story (which most Ranger fans already know) of how the Lone Ranger got started, how he obtained his great horse Silver, how he met his faithful Indian companion Tonto, and so on. Apparently the idea behind this version was to treat a children's fable (with which millions of adults grew up) in an adult manner, cashing in on the nostalgia craze of recent years. This approach succeeded with the Superman movies, but somehow didn't work as well with the Lone Ranger. Our warm memories don't include profanity, and unfortunately, this version of the Ranger story included some swear words.

A young actor named Klinton Spilsbury played the masked rider with less conviction than Clayton Moore and earlier actors. Michael Horse, whose name sounds authentic enough, plays a sort of urban, contemporary Tonto with none of the quiet dignity that Jay Silverheels gave to the role. The film tells how outlaws burn young John Reed's home, killing his parents. Tonto, a young Indian boy, brings him to his tribe, who cares for him. Reed later studies law in Detroit and joins his brother Dan, a member of the Texas Rangers, on a foray against an outlaw band. All the Rangers except John Reed are killed in an ambush. He meets Tonto again, who gives him silver bullets. He captures Silver, a great wild horse, and he's in business, with the purchase of a black mask. He gains revenge on the outlaws, of course, and rescues President U S Grant from them. The rest is history, if a bit fanciful. The photography is good, but it's not a good Western.

THE STARS

Literally thousands of movie actors have appeared in Westerns. Most of the biggest male stars of the screen have appeared in Westerns at one time or another in their careers and many of them have given excellent performances in this genre. It would require a book far larger than this one to present biographies of all the actors who have starred in Westerns. Instead, we have singled out some of the stars whose careers centered on Westerns—actors who are primarily identified with Westerns. Many of us grew up watching some of these stars in low-budget 'B' movies, which were a long way from being classics. But they, too, contributed to the amazing popularity and durability of Westerns in general.

One of the stars of John Wayne's film *The Alamo* (1960) was Laurence Harvey (center). The movie ran over three hours and cost some 12 million dollars, but most critics agreed that it was pretty boring, although the siege sequence was oustanding.

Autry, Gene (1907–)

Gene Autry's gigantic success in films stemmed from his being the first successful 'singing cowboy.' He and his studio producers invented the formula for a new type of cowboy hero for children—one who paused during his action-packed adventures to sing songs and play a guitar. Autry's breakthrough with this formula in the 30s was a revolution in 'B' Westerns that propelled him into the Top Ten Hollywood movie stars for box office appeal. Roy Rogers and many others imitated Autry, but he was the original and his career in movies, radio, television, recording and personal shows flourished until the 1960s. He had nine million-seller record hits, more than any of his imitators. Autry grew up in Texas and became a railroad telegrapher in Oklahoma. Will Rogers happened to stop at the station while Autry was singing and strumming his guitar one dull evening. He encouraged the young man and a Columbia Records scout soon signed him to a contract. Radio stardom soon followed, then movies. Autry's mellow singing voice and his famous horse, Champion, made him a superstar all over America and in Europe. When he wound up his performing career, Autry went on to be an even bigger success as a businessman. He is wealthier than any other star in Hollywood today.

Barry, Don 'Red' (1912–)

Donald Barry has never had red hair. The 'Red' was added to his billing to take advantage of his popularity as Red Ryder, a role he played in *The Adventures of Red Ryder*, a 'B' Western serial made in 1940 and 1941. His long career as a supporting player and a Western star began in the 30s. Barry plays supporting roles in movies and television today, but most of these roles are not in Westerns. A star athlete in Texas, Barry broke into movies after a stint in advertising. Small in stature, he projects a certain feistiness that some have compared with James Cagney. He has played in dozens of 'B' Westerns, some 'A' Westerns and a number of non-Western movies and TV shows. He has been able to play villains and heroes with equal ease. Still popular, Barry is frequently invited to appear at Western-film fan conventions.

Boyd, William (1895–1972)

The advent of television killed the 'B' Westerns in the 50s, but William Boyd was one star who prospered. Known to millions as Hopalong Cassidy, the role he played in many Saturday-matinee movies, he took this role to television and became a hero to a new generation of youngsters. Born in poverty in Ohio, Boyd worked at menial jobs until he broke into movies in 1918. He was featured in a number of comedies and swashbuckling adventure films in the silent era, including some for Cecil

Gene Autry.

Clint Eastwood, as the marshal in *Hang 'Em High* (1968), escorts Alan Hale Jr to jail.

Gary Cooper in his role in *North West Mounted Police* (1940).

B DeMille. Boyd's well-modulated voice helped him make the transition to sound films and he continued to star. He was known for his high living, drinking and gambling around Hollywood, but he soon had to change this image (at least on screen). In 1935, he signed a six-picture deal to play Hopalong Cassidy, a role he would play for the rest of his life. Hoppy, of course, didn't smoke, drink or swear on screen and hardly ever kissed the heroine. Boyd also insisted on minimizing the violence in Cassidy films and television shows. Hopalong Cassidy, dressed in black and riding his white horse, Topper, was an enormously popular hero to millions of youngsters for many years. Boyd bought the rights to the character and later sold his William Boyd Enterprises for $8 million—a successful end to a fabulous career.

Cooper, Gary (1901–1961)

Gary Cooper is considered by many to be one of the two greatest Western stars (along with John Wayne) in film history. One of Hollywood's giants, Cooper didn't specialize in Westerns, of course, but he made many of them. He won an Academy Award for his performance in the classic *High Noon*, an honor that is rare for Western actors. Cooper undoubtedly had more acting talent than most cowboy actors, and once his movie career was established, he appeared only in big-budget productions. Raised in Montana but educated in England and Iowa, Cooper was at home on a horse. He began his career as an extra in Tom Mix Westerns and other films. He changed his name from Frank Cooper to Gary on the advice of his first agent, who was born in Gary, Indiana. His career, which began in silent films in 1925, lasted until his death in 1961, netting him three Oscars and undying fame as a likeable and believable actor.

Eastwood, Clint (1930–   )

A box office star who doesn't specialize in Westerns, Eastwood nonetheless owes his superstar status to a form of the genre that he popularized: the 'Spaghetti Western.' After years of struggling as an actor with only mediocre success (including a TV series stint in *Rawhide*), Eastwood went to Europe to appear in *A Fistful of Dollars*, one of the first 'Spaghetti Westerns.' He was paid only $15,000 for his work and the film didn't appear in the US until two years later. But he quickly followed up with two more of these European Westerns and the public went wild over them. Eastwood played the deadliest, cold-blooded, most unkempt cowboy heroes the screen had seen until that time. He went on to direct and star in a number of Westerns and other films in the US after he became a superstar, creating violent, memorable characters such as 'Dirty Harry.' In recent years he has tried his hand at comedy roles. As a Western actor, Eastwood has added to the genre by taking the anti-hero to new heights of popularity in films.

Elliott, William 'Wild Bill' (1903–1965)

William Elliott is remembered as one of the better actors among the Western stars and though he appeared principally in 'B' Westerns, they were generally of better quality than most. Christened Gordon Nance, he began riding horses in his native Missouri when he was five and became a champion rodeo rider in his teens. When he entered films in 1925 after studying at the Pasadena Playhouse, he changed his name to Gordon Elliott. He spent many years playing small parts in all types of movies before gaining recognition in a Columbia serial, *The Great Adventures of Wild Bill Hickok*, in 1938. Changing his name again to Bill Elliott, he starred in many 'B' Westerns from then on. He played a strong, low-key cowboy and his trademark was the way he wore his two guns reversed in his holsters. In the 40s Republic billed him as 'Wild Bill' Elliott. He followed Don 'Red' Barry as Red Ryder in the serial of that name, and made a number of good cowboy films until his career was ended when the advent of television wiped out the 'B' Western in the 50s.

Gibson, Hoot (1892–1962)

Hoot Gibson was one of the biggest cowboy heroes to children in the 20s, behind William S Hart and Tom Mix. A former drifter, a champion rodeo rider and a very good movie stuntman, Gibson became a star in many short Westerns directed by John Ford. Moving on, he became an even bigger star with an immense following of youngsters, earning himself huge amounts of money. He spent the money as fast as he made it, on women, fast cars, motorcycles and airplanes. Gibson's breezy personality and flair for light comedy gave him an appealing screen personality. His films were packed with action but were light on violence. Gibson usually captured the villains without shooting them and he smiled a lot—unusual for a cowboy hero. He was never as successful in the sound era, though. His popularity waned in the 30s and his career ended in the early 40s. The big money he earned at the height of his career was all gone and he settled into a very modest retirement until his death in 1962.

Hart, William S (1870–1946)

William S Hart was one of the giants in the history of Western movies. He took the Western from the short one- and two-reelers of Broncho Billy Anderson and made it into full-length stories that depicted the Old West with realism and poetic feeling. He made silent Westerns that appealed to adults as well as children and he made them in his own way, putting his personal vision into each one. Acting as director and sometimes writer as well as star, Hart made films which achieved immense popularity and made him one of the most famous of all movie stars. Hart grew up in the Old West

William S Hart in *Hell's Hinges* (1916).

Ben Johnson in *The Last Picture Show* (1971).

66

Buck Jones.

and became a good Shakespearean stage actor in the East before making his first film in 1914. After 11 years of movie stardom, Hart retired when his sober, realistic Westerns began to fade in popularity behind the glamorized, action-filled, unrealistic films of Tom Mix. Hart just didn't want to change his style of movie. He had made his mark, and it's a great one.

Holt, Tim (1918–1973)

Tim Holt was the son of actor Jack Holt, who had a long career playing heroes and villains in Westerns. While the father rarely got beyond supporting parts, the son became a Western star. Tim Holt graduated from Culver Military Academy in Indiana with top grades before taking up his film career. His first Western was *The Law West of Tombstone* in 1938; a year later he had a good part in John Ford's classic *Stagecoach*, which made John Wayne a star. He went on to star in many better-than-average Westerns and also gave a fine performance in Orson Welles' *The Magnificent Ambersons* in 1942. Holt became a B-29 bombardier in World War II, winning many decorations for bravery in Pacific action. In 1948, he gave his best performance in *The Treasure of the Sierra Madre* with Humphrey Bogart and Walter Huston. This fine actor ended his film career in 1952 and became a rancher in Oklahoma. He did occasional radio and television work after that, and was also in the construction business for a while before his death in 1973.

Johnson, Ben (1922–   )

One of the most familiar faces in Westerns for the past 40 years, Ben Johnson has been in as many major sagebrush sagas as John Wayne. But until recent years, Johnson's name wasn't recognized by as many people as those of other actors. He has been a top-notch stuntman and a supporting actor (both as a villain and as a good guy) in many of the best Westerns made. He was a villain in *Shane*; he doubled for Henry Fonda in *Fort Apache* and for William Holden in *Horse Soldiers*; he was a featured actor with Wayne in *She Wore a Yellow Ribbon*, *Rio Lobo*, *Red River* and many other films. Johnson has nearly always appeared in top-quality productions; the list of his films reads like a list of Western classics. In 1972 Ben finally got the recognition he deserved: he won the Academy Award for Best Supporting Actor for his performance in *The Last Picture Show*. Billionaire Howard Hughes talked Johnson into leaving his Oklahoma ranch to go into movies and gave him a role in his production of *The Outlaw* in the 40s. The rest, as they say, is history.

Jones, Buck (1889–1942)

Born Charles Gebhart in Indiana, Buck Jones was a youngster when his family moved to Oklahoma. He learned ranch life and became a top rodeo rider and then joined the army. Jones later appeared as a trick rider with the Ringling Brothers circus before getting his start in movies as a bit player and stuntman. Fox studios built him up as a rival to their biggest star, Tom Mix, to keep Mix in line. Buck Jones then launched himself on a spectacular career as a 'B' Western star, becoming one of the handful of greatest stars in the 20s and 30s. Buck Jones was a better-than-average cowboy actor who developed a huge following among youngsters at Saturday matinees. He always appeared astride his white horse, Silver. He was still acting in 1942, although he was not the big star he had been earlier. In that year, he was killed in the Cocoanut Grove nightclub fire in Boston, which took nearly five hundred lives. Buck Jones died a hero's death, giving his own life to go back into the fire to save other people.

Maynard, Ken (1895–1973)

Along with Tom Mix, Buck Jones, Tim McCoy and Hoot Gibson, Ken Maynard was one of the Big Five Western stars of the 20s and 30s who inherited the mantle of William S Hart. Like the others in this group, Maynard was a star of 'B' Westerns aimed at youngsters. And like the others, he had a large and devoted following of young fans who idolized this hero in the white hat. Also like the others, he was a real cowboy, a rodeo performer and a trick rider with the circus before entering films. He taught the young John Wayne a lot about riding and stunting. Unfortunately, Maynard had a drinking problem that hastened the end of his career. He spent all the money he made as a star, and he ended his life living in a trailer, broke. But many fans still remember Ken Maynard and his magnificent horse, Tarzan, as heroes on the silver screen.

McCoy, Tim (1891–1978)

Another of the Big Five Western stars of the 20s and 30s, Tim McCoy was not only a real cowboy with a ranch in Wyoming, but an army officer as well. He served in combat in both World Wars. McCoy was a leading authority on Indian history and was better educated and more polished than his cowboy actor contemporaries. He left fulltime army life to enter the movies in 1923 as a technical consultant on the classic silent Western, *The Covered Wagon*. He was soon starring in Westerns and he proved to be a very popular 'B' Western star. As a historian of the Old West, he regretted that the cowboy movies didn't depict life as it really was, but he realized the primary goal of the films was entertainment. For more than 15 years, Tim McCoy was a hero to millions of youngsters in scores of films. Always immaculately dressed in his roles (in black), he wore oversized Stetsons and a pearl-handled gun. His career had evaporated when he returned from World War II, but he kept busy with cameo roles and by touring with a Wild West show right up to his death at the age of 86 in 1978. Tim

Top : Colonel Tim McCoy (second from right) in *Frontier Crusader*, was an advisor on *The Covered Wagon* (1923).

McCoy is remembered as one of the real gentlemen of Western films.

McCrea, Joel (1905–)

Most film critics would place Joel McCrea among the top stars in the history of quality Westerns. Indeed, McCrea has appeared only in high-quality Western films throughout his long career. A wealthy rancher today, he 'retired' from films some years ago only to keep coming out of retirement for special roles and guest spots in films and television. McCrea, along with his close friend, Randolph Scott, was known as a solid, 'old pro' performer in 'A' Westerns for decades. A native Californian, McCrea studied acting and got his start in movies as an extra. He worked with dogged determination until he was finally allowed to play a feature role in *The Jazz Age* in 1929. For the first 15 years of his career, McCrea appeared in comedies, spy films and adventure stories as well as Westerns. But after that he worked almost exclusively in Westerns, reaching the peak of his popularity in the 40s and 50s. He and Scott capped their fulltime screen careers in 1962 by teaming in the classic *Ride The High Country*, one of the best Westerns ever made.

Mix, Tom (1880–1940)

Universally hailed as 'the greatest cowboy star of them all,' Tom Mix was exactly that. His fame rests not on the quality of his films (they were low-budget films and serials aimed at juvenile audiences) nor on realistic portrayals of the West (Mix was the original fancy-dress cowboy hero, performing feats of derring-do that defied reality). But at the peak of his fame, Mix was better known than any cowboy star in history. Born in Pennsylvania, Mix was a champion rodeo rider, a soldier and a cowboy in Oklahoma before breaking into films. Studio publicists invented other wild adventures in his life—fighting in Cuba, the Philippines, the Boer War and serving as a Texas Ranger—which were false. Mix began in short Western films in 1914, with his horse Tony, who would become nearly as famous as Mix. Tom developed a formula of breezy, action-filled Westerns that was copied for decades afterward. He did all his own stunts and became 'the idol of every girl and boy in America.' He lived in a grandiose style, marrying five times and owning mansions and custom-made cars. When his career began to wane in the 30s, Mix earned large sums with his traveling circus. He died in a car crash in 1940, still famous.

Rogers, Roy (1912–)

Billed by Republic Studios and himself as 'King of the Cowboys,' Roy Rogers has been one of the most famous Western stars of all time, in movies, television and personal appearances. When Gene Autry, the number

Above : Tom Mix (1880–1940) almost always appeared with his horse, Tony. His first picture was made in 1910.

one 'B' Western star, enlisted in the army during World War II, Republic built a huge publicity campaign around Rogers, who didn't go into the service. Rogers went on to fame and fortune, marrying Dale Evans, the co-star of many of his films. Rogers had copied the Autry 'singing cowboy' formula in the late 30s, and his pleasant voice and personality enabled him to go far with it. Born in Ohio as Leonard Slye, he became a radio singer with a Western band, Bob Nolan and his Tumblin' Tumbleweeds (later known as the Sons of the Pioneers). He changed his movie name to Dick Weston in 1937 and to Roy Rogers in 1938 after small parts in a couple of Autry films and some other 'B' Westerns. As the wartime replacement for Autry, he wore even more outlandish costumes (looking like a 'Liberace of the plains') and became the idol of millions of children. He was equally successful in his television show of the 50s and does personal appearances today. Roy Rogers' wholesome image is still popular with millions of people.

Scott, Randolph (1903– 1987)

Randolph Scott has always looked like the quintessential Western hero, with his rugged face, athletic build and soft-spoken manner. In a long career, he became one of the most familiar and best-liked Western stars in high-quality productions. He contributed greatly to the genre with his solid, realistic portrayals of cowboys in scores of excellent films. At the height of his career, in the 50s, he was among the top box office stars in Hollywood, making superior films which withstood the competition of television. A Virginia-born true gentleman from an old Southern family, Scott broke into the movies in the late 20s and spent years working steadily without gaining top stardom. He came to true stardom in the 40s, making movies of all types but mostly Westerns. Working with John Wayne, Henry Fonda, Errol Flynn and others, Scott gained tremendous respect in Hollywood. His last film was his best, the classic *Ride the High Country*, made with his friend Joel McCrea in 1962. Scott retired after that film, and is one of the richest retired actors today.

Starrett, Charles (1904–   )

Charles Starrett holds the record for being a Western star the longest at a single studio (Columbia). He appeared in that studio's films from 1935 to 1952, winning fame along the way as 'The Durango Kid' at the height of his career. Born in Athol, Massachusetts and a graduate of Dartmouth, the good-looking, neatly dressed Starrett was a mainstay of 'B' Westerns for most of his career, although he started in non-Western films. The modest Starrett never had any pretensions that his 'B' Westerns were more than horse operas made for youngsters, but within this category, he was a solid professional star, making entertaining films that were most popular in the 40s. The Durango Kid was a masked hero, dressed in black with a white Stetson, who avenged

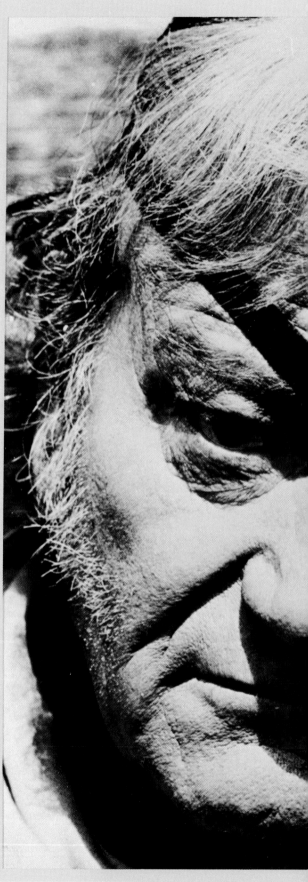

The late, great John 'Duke' Wayne, with his Rooster Cogburn eyepatch. He first made the list of the industry's ten top money-making stars in 1949, and remained on it until 1974.

wrongs wherever he happened to go. His sidekick was played by Smiley Burnette, who served in the same capacity with Gene Autry. From 1945 to his retirement in 1952, the Durango Kid role kept Starrett's name in the top ten Western box office stars. He lives in comfortable retirement today at Laguna Beach, California.

Wayne, John (1907–1979)

Almost any poll among movie fans or critics would show John Wayne to be the favorite Western actor. 'The Duke' was the very embodiment of the Western hero we always think of in the best-quality sagebrush sagas: tough, brave, loyal, honest and compassionate when the situation called for it. It is impossible to overstate Wayne's contributions to the Western genre during his career of half a century. He helped bring the Western film to its highest potential as a work of art, appearing in many classics. Wayne, whose real name was Marion Morrison, was an All-American football player for the University of Southern California before he got his start in films as a prop man, stuntman and extra. He 'paid his dues' for years in menial jobs and bit parts. His greatest friend and idol was director John Ford, who taught him discipline by criticizing him unmercifully in his early career days. Wayne's first good role was in *The Big Trail*, directed by Raoul Walsh in 1930. But Wayne hadn't become a very good actor at this point, and he spent nearly another decade struggling in mediocre films—some of them Westerns, some sea stories and other adventure films. But Wayne kept making progress and was gradually recognized as one of the leading Western actors. The movie that propelled him to stardom was John Ford's classic *Stagecoach*, made in 1939. Wayne's performance as Ringo in that film showed everyone that he could act and that he had star quality. His roles got larger after that and he continued to make Westerns, as well as war films, detective stories and adventure yarns through the 40s. But the next truly great Western he made didn't come along until 1948. He and Montgomery Clift starred in *Red River*, directed by Howard Hawks. This superb film was followed by a long string of excellent Westerns over the next quarter-century. Many of these Wayne vehicles would make almost anyone's list of the great Westerns in cinema history: *She Wore a Yellow Ribbon*; *Hondo*; *The Searchers*; *Rio Bravo*; *The Horse Soldiers*; *The Alamo*; *The Man Who Shot Liberty Valance*; *The Sons of Katie Elder*; *Eldorado*; *True Grit*; *Rooster Cogburn*; and *The Shootist*. Wayne finally received the recognition he had deserved for a long time when he won the Academy Award for Best Actor for his performance in *True Grit*. In Wayne's final film, *The Shootist*, made in 1976, he played an old gunfighter hero who is dying of cancer but who goes out in a blaze of glory. It was a fitting finale to the greatest career in Western screen history. John Wayne died of cancer three years later, a legendary hero to millions around the world.

Above : Cat Ballou (1965) was a spoof Western for which Lee Marvin received an Oscar as a town drunk and a gunfighter.

Opposite top : Bad Day at Black Rock (1955) starred Spencer Tracy and Anne Francis.

Opposite bottom : Broken Arrow (1950), starred James Stewart and Debra Paget.

FILMOGRAPHY

Key : D = director   S = stars

The Alamo
1960 (United Artists). D: John Wayne. S: John Wayne, Richard Widmark, Laurence Harvey, Richard Boone, Frankie Avalon, Linda Cristal.

Bad Day at Black Rock
1955 (MGM). D: John Sturges. S: Spencer Tracy, Anne Francis, Robert Ryan, Dean Jagger, Walter Brennan, Ernest Borgnine, Lee Marvin.

Broken Arrow
1950 (20th-Century-Fox). D: Delmer Daves. S: James Stewart, Jeff Chandler, Debra Paget, Basil Ruysdael, Will Geer.

Butch Cassidy and the Sundance Kid
1969 (20th-Century-Fox). D: George Roy Hill. S: Paul Newman, Robert Redford, Katharine Ross.

Cat Ballou
1965 (Columbia). D: Elliott Silverstein. S: Jane Fonda, Lee Marvin, Michael Callan, Dwayne Hickman, Nat King Cole, Stubby Kaye.

Cimarron
1931 (RKO). D: Wesley Ruggles. S: Richard Dix, Irene Dunne, Estelle Taylor, William Collier Jr, Rosco Ates.

The Covered Wagon
1923 (Paramount). D: James Cruz. S: Alan Hale, Lois Wilson, J Warren Kerrigan, Ernest Torrance.

Dark Command
1940 (Republic). D: Raoul Walsh. S: John Wayne, Claire Trevor, Walter Pidgeon, Roy Rogers, George 'Gabby' Hayes, Porter Hall, Marjorie Main.

Dodge City
1939 (Warner Bros). D: Michael Curtiz. S: Errol Flynn, Olivia de Havilland, Ann Sheridan, Bruce Cabot, Frank McHugh, Alan Hale.

Duel in the Sun
1946 (David O Selznick). D: King Vidor. S: Gregory Peck, Jennifer Jones, Joseph Cotten.

For a Few Dollars More
1965 (United Artists). D: Sergio Leone. S: Clint Eastwood, Lee Van Cleef, Gian Maria Volonte.

Fort Apache
1948 (RKO). D: John Ford. S: Henry Fonda, John Wayne, Shirley Temple, John Agar, Ward Bond.

The Girl of the Golden West
1938 (MGM). D: Robert Z Leonard. S: Nelson Eddy, Jeanette McDonald, Walter Pidgeon, Leo Carillo, Buddy Ebsen.

Go West
1925 (MGM). D: Buster Keaton. S: Buster Keaton, Kathleen Meyers, Howard Truesdale.

Go West
1940 (MGM). D: Edward Buzzell. S: The Marx Brothers (Groucho, Harpo, Chico), John Carroll, Diana Lewis.

The Great Northfield, Minnesota Raid
1972 (Universal). D: Philip Kaufman. S: Cliff Robertson, Robert Duvall, Luke Askew, R G Armstrong.

The Great Train Robbery
1903 (The Edison Company). D: Edwin S Porter. S: None.

Gunfight at the O.K. Corral
1957 (Paramount). D: John Sturges. S: Burt Lancaster, Kirk Douglas, Rhonda Fleming, Jo Van Fleet, John Ireland, Earl Holliman.

The Gunfighter
1950 (20th Century-Fox). D: Henry King. S: Gregory Peck, Helen Westcott, Millard Mitchell, Karl Malden, Skip Homeier, Richard Jaeckel.

Hang 'em High
1968 (United Artists). D: Ted Post. S: Clint Eastwood, Inger Stevens, Ed Begley, Pat Hingle.

Hell's Hinges
1916 (Triangle Pictures). D: William S Hart. S: William S Hart, Clara Williams.

High Noon
1952 (United Artists). D: Fred Zinnemann. S: Gary Cooper, Grace Kelly, Thomas Mitchell, Lloyd Bridges, Katy Jurado, Lon Chaney Jr.

Hombre
1967 (20th Century-Fox). D: Martin Ritt. S: Paul Newman, Frederic March, Richard Boone, Diane Cilento, Barbara Rush, Martin Balsam.

Hondo
1953 (Warner Bros). D: John Farrow. S: John Wayne, Geraldine Page, Ward Bond, James Arness, Michael Pate.

Hopalong Cassidy
1935 (Paramount). D: Howard Bretherton. S: William Boyd, Jimmy Ellison, Paula Stone, Robert Warwick, Charles Middleton.

Above: Robert Redford in a fight scene from *Jeremiah Johnson* (1972).

Top: One of America's great silent clowns, Buster Keaton, in *Go West* (1925).

Top: Gunfight at the O.K. Corral (1957) was another rehash of the Wyatt Earp Tombstone story. Here Wyatt (Burt Lancaster, second from left) and his two brothers head for the corral with Doc Holliday (Kirk Douglas, left).

How the West Was Won
1963 (MGM). D: Henry Hathaway, John Ford, George Marshall. S: Spencer Tracy, John Wayne, Henry Fonda, James Stewart, Gregory Peck, Richard Widmark, Robert Preston, Karl Malden, Carroll Baker, Lee J Cobb and many more stars.

Hud
1963 (Paramount). D: Martin Ritt. S: Paul Newman, Melvyn Douglas, Patricia Neal, Brandon de Wilde, John Ashley.

In Old Arizona
1929 (Fox). D: Raoul Walsh, Irving Cummings. S: Warner Baxter, Edmund Lowe, Dorothy Burgess, J Farrell McDonald.

The Iron Horse
1924 (Fox). D: John Ford. S: George O'Brien, Madge Bellamy.

Jeremiah Johnson
1972 (Warner Bros). D: Sydney Pollack. S: Robert Redford, Will Geer, Stefan Gierasch, Delle Bolton.

Jesse James
1939 (20th Century-Fox). D: Henry King. S: Henry Fonda, Tyrone Power, Nancy Kelly, Randolph Scott, Henry Hull.

Johnny Guitar
1954 (Republic). D: Nicholas Ray. S: Sterling Hayden, Joan Crawford, Mercedes McCambridge, Scott Brady, Ward Bond, Ernest Borgnine, John Carradine.

Last of the Mohicans
1936 (United Artists). D: George B Seitz. S: Randolph Scott, Binnie Barnes, Heather Angel, Hugh Buckler.

Law and Order
1932 (Universal). D: Edward Cahn. S: Walter Huston, Harry Carey, Raymond Hatton, Russell Simpson, Walter Brennan.

The Left-Handed Gun
1958 (Warner Bros). D: Arthur Penn. S: Paul Newman, Lita Milan, John Dehner, James Congdon, James Best.

The Life and Times of Judge Roy Bean
1972 (National General). D: John Huston. S: Paul Newman, Jacqueline Bisset, Ava Gardner, Tab Hunter, John Huston, Stacy Keach, Roddy McDowall, Anthony Perkins, Victoria Principal, Ned Beatty.

The Lone Ranger
1956 (Warner Bros). D: Stuart Heisler. S: Clayton Moore, Jay Silverheels, Lyle Bettger, Bonita Granville, Perry Lopez.

Lonely Are the Brave
1962 (Universal). D: David Miller. S: Kirk Douglas, Walter Matthau, Gena Rowlands, Carroll O'Connor, George Kennedy.

The Magnificent Seven
1960 (United Artists). D: John Sturges. S: Yul Brynner, Eli Wallach, Steve McQueen, Charles Bronson, Horst Buchholz, Robert Vaughn, James Coburn.

The Man from Laramie
1955 (Columbia). D: Anthony Mann. S: James Stewart, Arthur Kennedy, Donald Crisp, Cathy O'Donnell, Wallace Ford, Jack Elam.

My Darling Clementine
1946 (20th Century-Fox). D: John Ford. S: Henry Fonda, Linda Darnell, Victor Mature, Walter Brennan, Tim Holt, Ward Bond, Cathy Downs, John Ireland.

Northwest Mounted Police
1940 (Paramount). D: Cecil B De Mille. S: Gary Cooper, Madeleine Carroll, Paulette Goddard, Preston Foster, Robert Preston, George Bancroft, Lon Chaney Jr, Lynne Overman.

One Eyed Jacks
1961 (Paramount). D: Marlon Brando. S: Marlon Brando, Karl Malden, Pina Pellicer, Ben Johnson, Slim Pickens.

The Oklahoma Kid
1939 (Warner Bros). D: Lloyd Bacon. S: James Cagney, Humphrey Bogart, Rosemary Lane, Donald Crisp, Charles Middleton, Ward Bond.

The Outlaw Josey Wales
1976 (Warner Bros). D: Clint Eastwood. S: Clint Eastwood, Sondra Locke, John Vernon, Chief Dan George.

Above: Gary Cooper and Madeleine Carroll were two of the stars in *North West Mounted Police* (1940).

Opposite: It was rare that James Cagney played the part of a cowboy. Here he is in *The Oklahoma Kid* (1939).

Below: Despite his accent and exotic appearance, Yul Brynner (right) made a convincing cowboy—*The Magnificent Seven* (1960).

The Ox-Bow Incident
1943 (20th Century-Fox). D: William Wellman.
S: Henry Fonda, Dana Andrews, Mary Beth Hughes,
Anthony Quinn, Harry Morgan.

The Plainsman
1936 (Paramount). D: Cecil B De Mille. S: Gary
Cooper, Jean Arthur, James Ellison, Charles Bickford,
Porter Hall.

Red River
1948 (United Artists). D: Howard Hawks. S: John
Wayne, Montgomery Clift, Joanne Dru, Walter Brennan,
Coleen Gray, John Ireland, Noah Beery Jr.

Ride the High Country
1962 (MGM). D: Sam Peckinpah. S: Randolph Scott,
Joel McCrea, Mariette Hartley, James Drury, Ronald
Starr.

Rio Bravo
1959 (Warner Bros). D: Howard Hawks. S: John Wayne,
Dean Martin, Ricky Nelson, Angie Dickinson, Walter
Brennan, Ward Bond, John Russell, Claude Akins.

Rio Grande
1950 (Republic). D: John Ford. S: John Wayne,
Maureen O'Hara, Ben Johnson, Claude Jarman Jr.

Rooster Cogburn
1975 (Universal). D: Stuart Millar. S: John Wayne, Katharine Hepburn, John McIntyre, Richard Jordan.

Santa Fe Trail
1940 (Warner Bros). D: Michael Curtiz. S: Errol Flynn, Olivia de Havilland, Raymond Massey, Ronald Reagan, Alan Hale, Van Heflin.

The Searchers
1956 (Warner Bros). D: John Ford. S: John Wayne, Jeffrey Hunter, Vera Miles, Ward Bond, Natalie Wood, Harry Carey Jr.

Shane
1953 (Paramount). D: George Stevens. S: Alan Ladd, Jean Arthur, Van Heflin, Brandon de Wilde, Ben Johnson, Jack Palance, Elisha Cook Jr.

She Wore a Yellow Ribbon
1949 (RKO). D: John Ford. S: John Wayne, Joanne Dru, John Agar, Ben Johnson, Harry Carey Jr, Mildred Natwick, George O'Brien, Victor McLaglen.

The Spoilers
1942 (Universal). D: Ray Enright. S: Randolph Scott, John Wayne, Marlene Dietrich, Margaret Lindsay.

Stagecoach
1939 (United Artists). D: John Ford. S: John Wayne, Claire Trevor, Thomas Mitchell, John Carradine, Donald Meek, George Bancroft.

They Died With Their Boots On
1941 (Warner Bros). D: Raoul Walsh. S: Errol Flynn, Olivia De Havilland, Arthur Kennedy, Charles Grapewin, Gene Lockhart.

The Treasure of the Sierra Madre
1948 (Warner Bros). D: John Huston. S: Humphrey Bogart, Walter Huston, Tim Holt, Bruce Bennett, Barton MacLane.

True Grit
1969 (Paramount). D: Henry Hathaway. S: John Wayne, Kim Darby, Glen Campbell, Robert Duvall, Dennis Hopper, Strother Martin, Jeremy Slate.

Tom Horn
1980 (Warner Bros). D: William Wiard. S: Steve McQueen, Richard Farnsworth, Slim Pickens.

Tumbleweeds
1925 (United Artists); (re-release with prologue by William S Hart, Astor, 1939). D: King Baggott. S: William S Hart, Barbara Bedford, Lucien Littlefield, J Gordon Russell.

Union Pacific
1939 (Paramount). D: Cecil B De Mille. S: Barbara Stanwyck, Joel McCrea, Akim Tamiroff, Robert Preston, Lynne Overman.

Above : In *The Wild Bunch* (1969), a cynical band of outlaws fight law, order, and the Mexican Army on the Texas-Mexico border in 1913. These members of the gang are (left to right) Ben Johnson, Warren Oates, William Holden, Ernest Borgnine.

Opposite top : Humphrey Bogart (right), talks with one of his partners, Walter Huston, in a Mexican village in *The Treasure of the Sierra Madre* (1948). This story of thieves falling out over gold after an arduous search in bandit country won an Oscar for Huston and two for his son, John, for screenplay and direction.

Opposite bottom : Romance enters the life of Robert Preston when he falls in love with Barbara Stanwyck, the pretty postmistress at the end of the track. She holds him at arm's length despite luxurious presents, such as a fur coat. A scene from Cecil B De Mille's *Union Pacific* (1939).

The Virginian
1929 (Paramount). D: Victor Fleming. S: Gary Cooper, Walter Huston, Richard Arlen, Mary Brian, Chester Conklin.

Wagonmaster
1950 (RKO). D: John Ford. S: Ben Johnson, Harry Carey Jr, Joanne Dru, Ward Bond, Charles Kemper, Alan Mowbray.

Warlock
1959 (20th Century-Fox). D: Edward Dmytryk. S: Richard Widmark, Henry Fonda, Anthony Quinn, Dorothy Malone.

The Westerner
1940 (United Artists). D: William Wyler. S: Gary Cooper, Walter Brennan, Doris Davenport, Fred Stone, Paul Hurst, Chill Wills, Charles Halton, Forrest Tucker.

The Wild Bunch
1969 (Warner Bros–Seven Arts). D: Sam Peckinpah. S: William Holden, Ernest Borgnine, Robert Ryan, Edmund O'Brien, Warren Oates, Ben Johnson, Jaime Sanchez.

INDEX

Picture Credits